Advances in Computing Communications and Informatics

(Volume 6)

IoT-enabled Sensor Networks: Architecture, Methodologies, Security, and Futuristic Applications

Edited by

Samayveer Singh
Department of Computer Science and Engineering
Dr. B. R. Ambedkar National Institute of Technology
Jalandhar, Punjab, India

Manju
Department of Computer Science and Information Technology
Jaypee Institute of Information Technology
Noida, Uttar Pradesh, India

Aruna Malik
Department of Computer Science and Engineering
Dr. B. R. Ambedkar National Institute of Technology
Jalandhar, Punjab, India

&

Pradeep Kumar Singh
Jaypee University of Information Technology
Waknaghat, India

Advances in Computing Communications and Informatics

(Volume 6)

IoT-enabled Sensor Networks: Architecture, Methodologies, Security, and Futuristic Applications

Editors: Samayveer Singh, Manju, Aruna Malik and Pradeep Kumar Singh

ISSN (Online): 2737-5730

ISSN (Print): 2737-5722

ISBN (Online): 978-981-5049-48-0

ISBN (Print): 978-981-5049-49-7

ISBN (Paperback): 978-981-5049-50-3

First published in 2024.

need for a court order if at any point you breach any terms of this License Agreement. In no event will any delay or failure by Bentham Science Publishers in enforcing your compliance with this License Agreement constitute a waiver of any of its rights.

3. You acknowledge that you have read this License Agreement, and agree to be bound by its terms and conditions. To the extent that any other terms and conditions presented on any website of Bentham Science Publishers conflict with, or are inconsistent with, the terms and conditions set out in this License Agreement, you acknowledge that the terms and conditions set out in this License Agreement shall prevail.

Bentham Science Publishers Pte. Ltd.
80 Robinson Road #02-00
Singapore 068898
Singapore
Email: subscriptions@benthamscience.net

BENTHAM SCIENCE

CONTENTS

PREFACE

The Internet of Things (IoT) significantly broadens the use of information technology by fusing the physical and digital worlds. The third wave of the IT industry revolution is currently being led by futuristic device-based networking. When it comes to smart gadgets and embedded wireless technologies that use sensing devices, recent years have witnessed enormous growth. In the near future, it is expected that billions of devices need to be connected to the Internet directly or indirectly. The term "IoT", which was first proposed by Kevin Ashton, a British technologist, in 1999, has the potential to impact everything in today's world, right from health care, smart cities, education, and industries.

As equipment becomes more digitalized and interconnected, networks between machines, people, and the Internet are formed. This results in the development of new ecosystems that allow for increased productivity, improved energy efficiency, and increased profitability. Sensors help to recognize the state of things, by which they gain the advantage of anticipating human needs based on the information collected per context. These sophisticated devices can make decisions on their own without human assistance in addition to gathering information from their surroundings.

We can turn on the lights in our homes from a desk in an office miles away. The built-in cameras and sensors embedded in our refrigerator let us easily keep tabs on what is present on the shelves, and when an item is close to expiration. When we get home, the thermostat has already adjusted the temperature so that it's lukewarm or brisk, depending on our preference. These are merely a few of the millions of Internet of Things (IoT) frameworks in use these days. IoT has redefined the way we interact, communicate, and go about our daily work. From homes to maintenance to cities, the IoT ecosystem of devices is making our world smarter and more efficient. In this guide, we'll discuss everything you need to know about IoT, a world where more and more things are connected.

Chapters 1 and 2 of this book discuss in-depth the challenges, applications, and recent advances in the field of IoT. Chapters 3 to 5 have discussed various approaches to IoT implementation in different niches, along with an analysis of IoT-enabled wireless sensor networks. Chapters 6 and 9 provide information about recent technologies to mitigate security issues in IoT networks.

Samayveer Singh
Department of Computer Science and Engineering
Dr. B. R. Ambedkar National Institute of Technology
Jalandhar, Punjab, India

Manju
Department of Computer Science and Information Technology
Jaypee Institute of Information Technology
Noida, Uttar Pradesh, India   **Aruna Malik**
             Department of Computer Science and Engineering
             Dr. B. R. Ambedkar National Institute of Technology
             Jalandhar, Punjab, India

&

             Pradeep Kumar Singh
             Jaypee University of Information Technology
             Waknaghat, India

List of Contributors

Aatif Jamshed	ABES Engineering College, Ghaziabad, U.P., India
Ajay K. Sharma	Department of Computer Science and Engineering, National Institute of Technology Jalandhar, Jalandhar, Punjab, India
Aman Jatain	Department of Computer Science and Engineering, Amity University, Haryana, India
Amit Garg	IIMT Engineering College, Meerut, Uttar Pradesh, India Department of Computer Science, Manipal University, Jaipur, India
Anshu Kumar Dwivedi	Buddha Institute of Technology, Gorakhpur, U.P., India
Ankur Rastogi	Jain University, Bengaluru, Karnataka, India
Ankur	Department of Computer Science and Engineering, National Institute of Technology Jalandhar, Jalandhar, Punjab, India
Aruna Malik	Department of Computer Science and Engineering, Dr. B. R. Ambedkar National Institute of Technology, Jalandhar, Punjab, India
Arvind Dagur	Galgotias University, Greater Noida, U.P., India
Ashish Kumar	ITS Engineering College, Greater Noida, Uttar Pradesh, India
Deepti Singh	Department of Computer Science and Engineering, Netaji Subhas Institute of Technology (NSIT), Delhi, India
Manju	Department of Computer Science and Information Technology, Jaypee Institute of Information Technology, Noida, Uttar Pradesh, India
Pawan Singh Mehra	Delhi Technological University, New Delhi, India
Priyanshi Pandey	Department of Computer Science and Information Technology, Jaypee Institute of Information Technology, Noida, Uttar Pradesh, India
Suman Pandey	Department of Computer Science and Engineering, Kamla Nehru Institute of Technology (KNIT), Sultanpur, India
Sarika Chaudhary	Manav Rachna International Institute of Research and Studies (MRIIRS), Faridabad, Mohali, India
Samayveer Singh	Department of Computer Science and Engineering, Dr. B. R. Ambedkar National Institute of Technology, Jalandhar, Punjab, India
Saurabh Singhal	Department of Computer Science and Engineering, Apex Institute of Technology, Chandigarh University, Chandigarh, India
Ved Prakash	Department of Computer Science and Engineering, Kamla Nehru Institute of Technology (KNIT), Sultanpur, India
Vikas Verma	iNurture, Teerthanker Mahaveer University, Moradabad, Uttar Pradesh, India

CHAPTER 1

Internet-of-Things-Enabled Sensor Networks: Vision Challenges and Smart Applications

Aatif Jamshed[1]**, Anshu Kumar Dwivedi**[2]**, Pawan Singh Mehra**[3,*] **and Arvind Dagur**[4]

[1] *ABES Engineering College, Ghaziabad, U.P., India*

[2] *Buddha Institute of Technology, Gorakhpur, U.P., India*

[3] *Delhi Technological University, New Delhi, India*

[4] *Galgotias University, Greater Noida, U.P., India*

Abstract: Internet-of-Things is the future of connectivity that has turned the physical world into smart objects. The practical feature of Internet-of-Things is to combine all objects, rendering them dependent on a shared infrastructure, in such a manner that humans can regulate them as well as monitor their status. Internet-of-Things is a physical object network that is embedded with hardware, software, sensors, and networking to allow objects to share data with the connected devices. This chapter details the Internet of Things, vision challenges, and various intelligent applications in sensor-enabled networks. The wide-scale application of the Internet would significantly affect how computers and objects engage in real-life scenarios. This chapter aims to highlight the perspective of some novel technologies and innovative implementations for the protection, welfare, and privacy concerns due to the Internet of Things. Some critical sensor networks, which represent the most used sensor networks in many domains, such as Smart Applications, are included in this introduction section. A literature study on Internet-of-Things has been conducted for different aspects, such as infrastructure, implementation problems, *etc.* The authors offer several other applications that are significant. Future research directions for Internet-of-Things have been outlined in the study to equip novel researchers with the assessment of current status and to build upon them with creative ideas.

Keywords: Actuators, Internet-of-Things, Innovative homes, Sensors, Smart city, WSNs.

1. INTRODUCTION

The Internet of Things (IoT) is a network of physical devices and products used daily and connected to the Internet. It is interlinked with a multitude of devices

---

* **Corresponding author Pawan Singh Mehra:** Delhi Technological University, New Delhi, India; E-mail: pawansinghmehra@gmail.com

Samayveer Singh , Manju, Aruna Malik, and Pradeep Kumar Singh (Eds.)

that communicate with one another through the use of sensors, actuators, and processors, among other means. The Internet of Things aims to reach high levels of intelligence with the least amount of human contact possible [1, 2]. Many elements of life are made more pleasant by the Internet of Things (IoT), which adds automation and intelligence to many parts of existence. In this context, things are made self-aware and capable of making intelligent decisions on their own, making them more pleasant. There are a large number of heterogeneous devices in the Internet of Things that are all linked over a network. The Internet of Things (IoT) now covers a wide variety of applications, with services accessible in various industries, including manufacturing, healthcare, transport, farming, and smart home. A smart city encompasses all societal areas that rely on information and communication technology (ICTs) [3]. It also encompasses many applications, making city services and surveillance more aware, interactive, and effective. The backbone of Internet-of-Things [3] is the wireless sensor network (WSN), without which the notion of a smart city cannot be achieved. The devices interacting with the physical environment and imposing changes are known as sensors and actuators. Many devices are networked together *via* sensors in a heterogeneous environment, generating a vast and enormous volume. This data is saved and evaluated to extract knowledge and help decision-making [4]. A smart city comprises a diverse range of gadgets, including a mart and basic essentials. Due to the enormous number of sensors linked to the items, a great sign of data is collected. In the case of an intelligent city, the Internet-of-Things network must be scalable since it may be necessary to add new devices and delete old ones at any time and from any location. Incorporating WSNs is difficult due to the wide range of applications and technological differences across devices [5]. The fundamental a basic problem with the Internet: We must develop cities that are private and secure; which are adaptive, independent, reliable; and which are responsive and dependable. The complex is growing in developing cities due to intelligence in smart infrastructure, and these include issues like a lack of interoperability, context sensitivity, scalability, and managing enormous amounts of informatics pics as well as issues such as security, privacy, and integrity, as well as dynamic adaptation, dependability, and latency. To do this, the city takes care of every facet of society, using a diverse array of applications. As shown smart city's main components are comprised, the city is made up of different sectors of society. A smart city is a city that has several essential and interdependent healthcare, industry, transportation, agriculture, and home automation. The intelligent smart uses many factors like intelligent TechnoMarine governance. It also includes a range of facilities and technologies to make people easier in several applications. Internet-of-Things is transforming the education industry as smart city security requirements [6]. The Internet of Things (IoT) will transform the Internet in such a way that machine-to-machine (M2M) learning will become a reality [7]. As a solid backbone, the Internet infrastructure will exist. The reconfiguration will occur by making physical equipment 'smart,' allowing them to accomplish things on their own, giving rise to the 'Internet of Things.' The Internet of Items (Internet-of-Things) promises to make smart technologies more accessible by linking things at any time and in any location. The Internet of Things (IoT) idea was created in 1998, and Kevin Ashton coined the phrase in 1999 [8, 9]. Internet-of-Things essentially enables the interaction of real-world objects to be autonomous but secure [10]. The Internet of Things (IoT) decreases physical labor by automating routine tasks [11]. The number of items linked to the Internet is continuously increasing. Smartphones have a variety of sensors and actuators that collect data, execute computations on it, and then send the important data acquired through the Internet [11]. The authors will be able to construct many fresh applications that will lead to persuasive benefits by employing such a network with various devices containing the sensors [12]. Internet-of-Things smart things may be uniquely recognized. Radio-Frequency Identification (RFID) tags or barcodes are used on these devices, which are detected by sensor devices [13, 14]. The sensors send the collected data to the processing unit through the Internet for processing. The results of the processing are conveyed to the decision-making and action-invoking system, which then takes the required action.

1.1. Major Issues Resolved by Internet of Things

One of the main ideas behind the Internet of Things is to bring information from different devices together. However, this can only be done perfectly if the right information is given at the right time. This can be done with the help of Augmented Reality, which lets you use a headset or mobile device to see relevant and actionable data over your environment whenever you need to. Microsoft, NASA, Volvo, Autodesk, and Caterpillar are just a few of the big companies that have put a lot of money into AR. Autodesk and NASA have tried out different ways to use Microsoft's Hololens.

To explain this further, the following are the real world problems that IoT could help solve.

- IoT and AI can be used to find out what went wrong with a machine and how to fix it. This can be shown with the help of a centrifugal pump as an example. Real-time sensors will keep an eye on how the machine is working and pick up on any problems. When they do, real-time CFD analysis will be used to find out what went wrong. With AR, a real-time image or CAD diagram can be shown on top of the pump to show exactly what needs to be done to fix it.

- Technical documents assembly "A picture is worth 1,000 words". This saying is especially true when it comes to putting things together. User manuals and technical documents can make simple tasks harder than they need to be, like putting together industrial equipment in the same way over and over again. They can also be used to show videos of real assembly steps that were taken before, either by the person putting it together or by another worker.
- Smartphones and health equipment work together to instantly diagnose medical issues. You can get diagnostics and capture pictures to share with medical professionals all across the world. They enable the cost-effective collecting and distribution of data; enable inventors to consider application cases; create a digital power grid; play around with the delivery of energy. You will receive an energy profile from each device in your home. The digitalization of equipment will help businesses and enable the subsequent wave of digitization.
- It has the ability to keep an eye on substation security, track current electrical usage data, and report any anomalies promptly; the capacity to solve issues outside of one's silo in a utility where IT, Operations, and Security don't communicate; encourages communication regarding crucial topics.

2. RELATED WORK

The Internet of Things (Internet-of-Things) can be thought of as a large network structure made up of numerous linked real-world items that rely on sensory, communication, networking, and information-processing technologies. RFID is the foundation for Internet-of-Things, as it allows microchips to send identifying data to a reader through a wireless channel. Anyone may use RFID to analyze, track, and monitor items that have RFID tags attached to them [15]. Wireless Sensor Networks (WSNs) [16], another key technology, focus on intelligent sensors for sensing and monitoring. Since the 1980s, RFID has been used in the transit of products to customers, the manufacture of pharmaceutical items, and retail [17, 18], while WSN has been used in traffic, healthcare, and industrial monitoring [19, 20]. The expansion of Internet-of-Things is accelerated by advancements in both technologies. Other technologies and gadgets, including barcodes, location-based services, service-oriented architecture, near-field communication, Wimax, ZigBee, cloud computing, and so on, are being utilized to build a complete network to enable Internet-of-Things [21] (Fig. **1**).

2.1. Smart City's Architecture

Architecture is required to allow and resolve the key problems encountered by the Internet in the Internet-of-Things fields of services and their operations. The Internet of Things (Internet-of-Things) provides a level of abstraction, giving

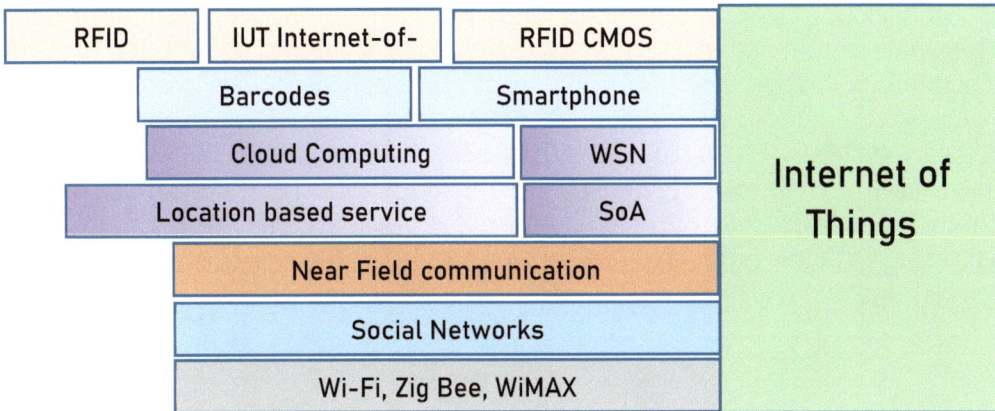

Fig. (1). Technologies empowering Internet-of-Things [19].

users access to physical devices and services while also allowing for device interoperability. An impressive number of things, ranging from refrigerators to light bulbs, may be connected to the Internet of Things (Internet-of-Things) with several purposes, capacities, features, and Internet protocols. A complex system of connected devices is implemented in an intelligent city Internet-of-Things framework. The device we are developing has a variety of sensors, which include different levels of both hardware and software heterogeneity. Thus, we want a flexible design that can accommodate both hardware and software variability. To illustrate this, imagine an intelligent urban Internet-of-Things system where information is exchanged not just amongst social applications but also with the government and management sectors as well. Cross-application services are essential for intelligent cities as they must, at any point in time, regardless of their size, be able to expand to various devices utilizing a range of technologies. The authors [22] argue that some domains in smart cities need to react promptly in real-time to well-structured resource planning, helping to effectively utilize available resources. Data management, communication issues due to the existence of many protocols, real-time processing of data, data protection, and privacy [23], as well as expansion of existing applications because of advancements in technology and greater use, all referred to as scalability [24] are necessary for standardized architectures to address common issues. Due to the diversity of devices, the dynamic nature of the network, and the requirement for scalability, security in all Internet-of-Things applications is one of the most demanding problems, especially in smart cities, where intercourse exists across numerous applications. Existing Internet-of-Things solutions do not fully fulfill the security requirements. Certain techniques are quite energy-intensive and hence expensive [22]. This type of architecture, seen in Fig. (**2**), is an open design that may handle a wide range of uses. It also shows that separate sectors are equipped with sensors and connected to one gateway to communicate information across different sectors, therefore assisting one another. In addition, the processing needs of the architecture to support Internet-of-Things problems, such as data processing, will be done on the edges of the device itself to serve essential applications like the healthcare system. Certain data, often known as fog computing, cannot be handled at the end of this software [25]. The conclusion drawn from the examination of architectural issues and the knowledge of the requirements for architecture in smart cities is that a smart city requires an open, flexible architecture that allows for scalability and extensibility.

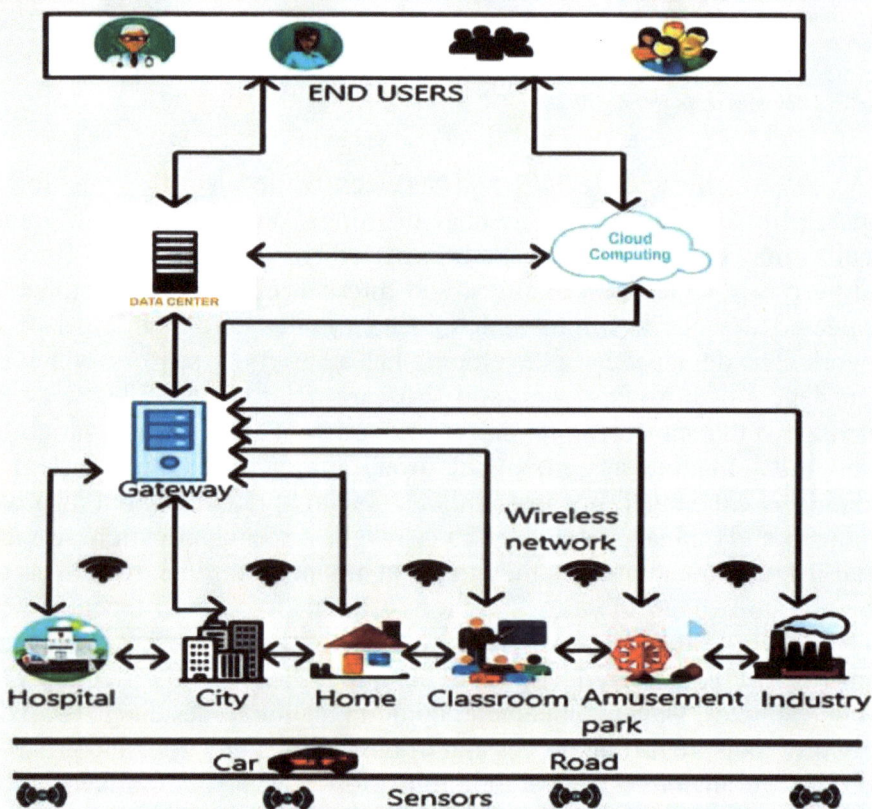

Fig. (2). The overall Internet-of-Things-based architecture of a smart city.

In other words, an additional large number of devices can be added to the system at any time. One must also take into consideration the scalability and diversity of the gadgets. An architectural framework is provided that is constructed on edge, with several direct and indirect ways of data connectivity for real-time data processing, as well as latency concerns that may be handled.

3. INTELLIGENT OR SMART CITY PLATFORM

As a vast amount of data is created by sensors, the smart city employs new technologies such as WSN: wireless sensor networks, and big data analytics to minimize resource use and provide intelligence to applications. Because data accumulates at a quick rate, and edge devices must manage comparable high computational and processing requirements, effective data storage is also necessary [26, 27].

3.1. Internet-of-Things Application Requirements

It is necessary to construct applications to apply Internet-of-Things solutions. However, the application implementation necessitates the following essential requirements:

1. One of the most important requirements of the Internet of Things is scalability. The platform should allow for the addition of any number of devices at any moment without affecting the application.

2. Internet-of-Things applications must be safe and reliable. As information travels in a variety of formats *via* the sensor network, these are the fundamental components.

3. Internet-of-Things applications require a self-adaptive system that optimizes its performance and can be adjusted to meet the changing requirements of the environment.

4. Internet of Things applications should be able to detect a situation and emotion depending on the context, personalize the services, and make judgments.

3.2. Internet-of-Things-Integrated Smart City WSN Applications and Roles

In every element of contemporary society, including e-health, e-transportation, energy, environment, and education, smart cities are transforming and altering the way we live and work. Using data from the meteorological department, for example, might be extremely beneficial in monitoring the environment, floods, and agricultural production. It may also be advantageous to monitor the health of old individuals and patients in the real world if done properly.

The following are some of the application domains where Internet-of-Things provides a significant benefit:

3.2.1. Internet-of-Things in Healthcare

Healthcare is being transformed by the Internet of Things, and it is one of the most significant and crucial applications in society. To increase the capabilities of healthcare structures as well as real-time monitoring and processing, wireless sensor networks are being used to achieve one of the most challenging goals. The key issues are lowering costs and enhancing patient care while also coping with a staffing shortage [28, 29].

3.2.1.1. Challenges for Internet-of-Things in Healthcare Industry

Internet-of-Things in healthcare gives patients and the elderly fresh hope, but achieving a seamless link between sites, patients, and hospitals is difficult. The following are the major roadblocks to Internet-of-Things integration in healthcare:

1. In the healthcare system, there is a lot of data to manage. A vast number of medical sensors are mounted on and around the patients [30]. The body's dynamic nature, with its constant state changes, makes it more difficult. As a result, gathering and evaluating data with precision becomes difficult.

2. Data is gathered in a variety of formats, including pictures acquired by cameras, changes and vibrations acquired by sensors, and body temperature acquired by sensors, among others. Bringing all of this data together and evaluating it on a single platform becomes a challenge.

3.2.2. Internet-of-Things in Industries

The industrial revolution is being ushered in by the Internet of Things (Internet-of-Things), which is facilitating more intermachine and interhuman communication as well as infusing intelligence into the value chain of a system, transforming it into a smart value chain. Industries are integrating intelligence and network connectivity throughout their process belts to improve their systems and goods. The advantages of integrating the Internet of Things include the ability to verify events, provide error alerts, and develop ideas to upgrade and replace current hardware, refineries, and offices with Internet-of-Things applications to boost the efficiency of the current system, among others.

- Incorporating machine learning (ML) and natural language processing (NLP) into industries to provide smart handling of equipment and premaintenance are the primary reasons for integrating the Internet of Things (Internet-of-Things) into their operations to provide their customers with new sets of premium services.

- Increasing efficiency and lowering processing costs by making pricing dynamic and evaluating data depending on consumption and sending it to the industrial value chain.
- In the retail industry, providing a tailored experience for both retailers and customers [27].

3.2.2.1. Challenges for Internet-of-Things in Industry

To help the healthcare system overcome its current scaling difficulties, the Internet of Things tackles some of the challenges that the healthcare system faces, such as system capacity, expansion in terms of capacity, and system and network size. The Internet-of-Things framework must be able to keep up with industries' infrastructure and operations, which are continuously increasing. It is due to the nature of the industry being organized into various divisions, such as manufacturing being different from retail and logistics, and IT being different from manufacturing. The gap in technical standards occurs when several pieces of hardware are involved in the technology or platform. In the world of Internet-o--Things-based goods, random designs are employed because companies are comfortable with them and because they have few norms to worry about. When more devices and platforms are in use, interoperability becomes a challenge. Because this hardware uses multiple applications to transport and utilize data, and bigger software architecture on the network and background servers will be required to deal with smart objects and provide support services, it will be necessary to build a bigger software architecture for it [31].

Fault tolerance is a critical issue for Internet-of-Things devices since they are dynamic and movable. Their conditions and behavior are continuously fluctuating. It is important to have a system in place for the Internet of Things (Internet-of-Things) and be able to adjust automatically in response to changes.

3.2.3. Internet of Things in Agriculture

Technology has lately revolutionized agriculture. Over the past several decades, technological innovation and industry have evolved to give more and better benefits to farmers. Agriculture has progressed to the point where farmers have absolute control over everything from crop production to sales. A collection of technologies known as the Internet of Things (IoT) has enabled a revolution in agriculture [32]. Researchers and scientific groups are working hard to develop Internet-of-Things applications that are coupled with wireless sensor networks (WSNs) for use in agriculture [33], and these projects continue to advance each day.

3.2.3.1. Challenges for Internet of Things in Agriculture

Because of the broad area, the effective application of Internet-of-Things in agriculture necessitates the deployment of a high number of Internet-of-Things devices, which might create interference with local spectra such as ZigBee, Wi-Fi, Sigfox, and LoRa [34]. Another difficulty is exposing the devices to adverse environmental conditions, such as physical damage and deterioration.

3.2.4. Homes or Buildings Integrated with Internet-of-Things

A smart home or building uses Internet-connected devices and items for remote monitoring of common household appliances such as lighting and water usage and monitoring and optimizing electrical equipment. Not only are day-to-day gadgets like smart doors and lighting managed with the smart homes and building idea, but the security of the house and building is also monitored. More home protection is provided through IP-based cameras, alarms, motion sensors, firefighting equipment, and connected door locks. Internet-of-Things-connected wireless sensors are bringing the revolution to deliver such automation in homes and businesses. Smart homes function by automating the home and its equipment, reducing the amount of user input required to operate them. Arduino, which uses sensors and actuators to develop smart home applications, is one of the most popular hardware platforms, while Zigbee technology is commonly used for networking.

3.2.4.1. Challenges for Internet-of-Things in Home and Building Structure

One of the issues of smart homes and buildings is heterogeneity across Internet-of-Things gadgets; the Internet-of-Things should be capable of effortlessly integrating different devices. Proposing a universal Internet-of-Things architecture for a smart city is difficult because of the enormous number and variety of devices, protocols, and services [35]. Interoperability refers to the capacity to connect devices at any time and from any location in an Iamnet-o--Things system. It is a major worry with smart home gadgets, and because each vendor's network infrastructure is distinct, achieving interoperability is difficult. To accomplish self-maintenance and management in Internet-of-Things smart homes and buildings, equipment should be capable of self-monitoring to improve their health and inform the user [36, 37].

3.2.5. Intelligent Transport System

The Internet of Things (IoT) is playing an increasingly important role in smart transportation, bringing solutions to a variety of challenges and enabling

Intelligent Transportation Systems. Several challenges exist in transportation applications, such as traffic congestion management and minimizing the environmental effect due to pollution to provide transportation advantages to business users and the general public. Vehicle intercommunication software can be supplied to assist inhabitants in saving time to create a smarter city. Intelligent Transportation System (ITS) [38] aims to improve traffic management by decreasing traffic congestion, providing real-time traffic information, local convenience, seat availability, and other features that benefit commuters while also improving their safety and comfort.

3.2.5.1. Challenges for Internet-of-Things in Smart Transport Systems

In an area where cloud computing centers are used in a smart transport system, a substantial number of automobiles are connected *via* Internet-of-Things; large amounts of data are generated and transmitted. Large quantities of data are processed and analyzed. The delay problem stems from the large amount of data gathered and processed, which in the case of a medical emergency, is harmful. The above problem is solved in Fog computing through real-time large data analysis at the middleware level and the node edge, but because intelligent transportation systems are dynamic, it is difficult to implement this solution, as well as heterogeneity in the large volume of Big Data collected *via* the transport system [39, 40].

3.2.6. Efficient Energy Management Using Internet-of-Things

The most pressing problem of modern civilization is the efficient use and management of energy. To use Internet-of-Things to make a city smart, a large number of Internet-of-Things-enabled applications are required. As the quantity and functionality of Internet-of-Things devices rise, so does the demand for power to control them. The effective use of energy is a critical need of the smart city. Smart houses and buildings, including schools, workplaces, amusement parks, roadways, and street lights, among others, have their energy usage data gathered and evaluated for optimization, as well as sent to the grid system for efficient resource use. Energy consumption may be reduced by effectively managing household appliances, education, and the healthcare system, according to the authors of [41]. Big data is collected from homes, businesses, and industries to regulate their energy use through the use of various processing algorithms and analyses.

3.2.6.1. Challenges for Internet of Things in Effective Energy Management

Several sorts of assaults may be perpetrated on smart homes and buildings, such as spoofing of identity, which attempts to use the energy of anybody for themselves. Eavesdropping is another attack against Internet-of-Things-based smart grids because information about the user and residential energy usage is used over the public communication infrastructure. Data management allows attackers to change the transmitted data to impact energy prices. The attackers can access and manage permissions by altering the measurements of smart meters and sensors and by remotely monitoring and modifying energy usage information. User's private information, including this, can be watched by analyzing use data [42].

3.2.7. Smart or Intelligent Water Management

Smart or intelligent water management refers to a set of procedures for efficiently managing water supply and usage to minimize waste. We all know that water scarcity is a major concern in society; the government investigated these difficulties, as well as equipment upkeep. Everyone interacts with the water management system, such as water resources, society, and environmental systems. The water management system is delicate, and it is always changing and growing as a result of many sectors ranging from industry to agriculture, each with its own set of requirements. Water consumption is the largest consumer in agriculture [43, 44], with leaks in distribution and irrigation being the primary causes of water waste. Furthermore, issues like under-irrigation and over-irrigation must be addressed. In agriculture, the Internet of Things necessitates the integration of a large number of devices, as well as items with diverse and complex sensors. The initiative includes cloud computing, big data analytics, and a new software package.

3.2.7.1. Challenges for Internet-of-Things in Water Management

One of the biggest problems in the case of water management is the risk of a physical attack on the equipment, which makes it simple to get most of the equipment. They may be copied by placing any malware or software on the devices [45]. Water is a resource that gives life, and water management is affected by interoperability and a lack of standardization in monitoring and equipment.

3.2.8. Monitoring of the Environment with Internet-of-Things

Using infrared wireless technology, the author proposed microcontroller-based waste bins or dustbins [46], which will display the present status of the waste on a mobile web browser and warn the user when the dustbins are full. When it comes to environmental hazards, air pollution is among the most significant. The main reasons for this are industrialization and the emissions of hazardous gases from vehicles; thus, the detection of the pollutant requires real-time monitoring [14]. Pollution is a solution to the air pollution problem presented by this research on the Internet of Things (Internet-of-Things). In combination with an Arduino-based air pollution monitoring system, a cloud-based platform for storing data from multiple external sensors is employed. The air Quality Assay of Carbon Monoxide, Carbon Dioxide, Nitrogen Dioxide, Methanol, Ozone, Ammonia, and Particulate Substance, Benzene, Ethanols, Toluene, and Propane will be evaluated in the following components. Carbon monoxide is the most harmful of the pollutants tested. In real-time environmental monitoring, such as environmental catastrophes and live monitoring, wireless sensor networks (WSN) are aided in the measurement of environmental parameters.

Alphonsa *et al*. [47] offered a method for the detection of landslides *via* Raspberry Pi-based Thing of the Internet. When video streaming data is received by a computer vision system, notifications are sent to an Android application. The authors of [48] suggested the Internet of Things and Wide Area Networks Early Warning System (WSN). Under the ground surface, the sensors are implanted. During earthquakes, a compression P wave and a transverse S wave are generated, on which the system is built. Since P waves move quicker, warning humans and automated electronic systems to take precautionary actions using waves are provided *via* earlier alarm signals. To broadcast warning signals, Zigbee transmitters are utilized, whereas smartphones are utilized to deliver warning texts.

3.2.8.1. Challenges for Internet-of-Things in Environmental Monitoring

It is necessary to meet various standards, such as product compatibility, to make good use of the Internet of Things to create a smart environment. A huge amount of data is created, which must be the top priority for the storage, access, and processing of these vast quantities of data created by the devices in the Internet-of-Things environment.

CONCLUSION

The Internet of Things is an emergent concept that has the potential to improve our daily lives by linking smart items, technology, and applications. The Internet of Things (IoT) would automate practically all of our daily routines. This chapter outlines the concept, the technology that enables it, its vision, and several potential applications. This should transmit good information and serve as a foundation for academics interested in the Internet of Things, essential technologies, and architecture. In addition, potential applications have been addressed. The problems are also briefly covered to provide an understanding of the obstacles that must be overcome for Internet-of-Things to become a reality.

In this chapter, the key concerns and problems in the deployment of Internet-of-Things applications are examined in depth. The research findings show that all applications linked to integrating WSN into the Internet of Things are faced with several common challenges (Internet-of-Things). Following this, information on the execution and functioning of the key sensors that are used in the applications is described. An open and flexible architecture may also be suggested that allows the architecture to be flexible and open while being heterogeneous and scalable. This chapter will assist academics in better understanding how wireless sensors represent the actual world of objects and objects that are connected to the network *via* which they communicate.

REFERENCES

[1]   P. Sethi, and S. R. Sarangi, "Internet of Things: Architectures, protocols, and applications", *J. Elect. Comp. Eng.,* 2017.
[http://dx.doi.org/10.1155/2017/9324035]

[2]   A.K. Dwivedi, A.K. Sharma, and R. Kumar, "Dynamic trust management model for the internet of things and smart sensors: The challenges and applications", *Recent Pat. Comput. Sci.,* vol. 12, 2019.

[3]   J. Jin, J. Gubbi, S. Marusic, and M. Palaniswami, "An information framework for creating a smart city through the internet of things", *IEEE Internet Things J.,* vol. 1, no. 2, pp. 112-121, 2014.
[http://dx.doi.org/10.1109/JIOT.2013.2296516]

[4]   A. Kumar Dwivedi, A. Kumar Sharma, and P. Singh Mehra, "Energy efficient sensor node deployment scheme for two stage routing protocol of wireless sensor networks assisted IoT", *ECTI Transactions on Electrical Engineering, Electronics, and Communications,* vol. 18, no. 2, pp. 158-169, 2020.
[http://dx.doi.org/10.37936/ecti-eec.2020182.240541]

[5]   P.S. Mehra, M.N. Doja, and B. Alam, "Zonal based approach for clustering in heterogeneous WSN", *Int. J. Inf. Technol.,* no. Dec, pp. 1-9, 2017.

[6]   S. Talari, M. Shafie-khah, P. Siano, V. Loia, A. Tommasetti, and J. Catalão, "A review of smart cities based on the internet of things concept", *Energies,* vol. 10, no. 4, p. 421, 2017.
[http://dx.doi.org/10.3390/en10040421]

[7]   Y. Huang, and G. Li, "Descriptive models for the internet of things", *Proceedings of 2010 International Conference on Intelligent Control and Information Processing, ICICIP 2010,* pp.483-486, 2010.
[http://dx.doi.org/10.1109/ICICIP.2010.5564232]

[8]   P. Gope, and T. Hwang, "Untraceable sensor movement in distributed IoT infrastructure", *IEEE Sens. J.,* vol. 15, no. 9, pp. 5340-5348, 2015.
[http://dx.doi.org/10.1109/JSEN.2015.2441113]

[9]   S. Singh, "Energy efficient multilevel network model for heterogeneous WSNs", *Eng. Sci. Technol. Int. J.,* vol. 20, no. 1, pp. 105-115, 2017.
[http://dx.doi.org/10.1016/j.jestch.2016.09.008]

[10]   T. Fan, and Y. Chen, "A scheme of data management in the internet of things", *2010 2ⁿᵈ IEEE International Conference on Network Infrastructure and Digital Content,* Beijing, China, 2010, pp. 110-114.
[http://dx.doi.org/10.1109/ICNIDC.2010.5657908]

[11]   Y. Huang, and G. Li, "A semantic analysis for internet of things", *2010 International Conference on Intelligent Computation Technology and Automation, ICICTA 2010,* vol. 1, pp. 336-339, 2010.
[http://dx.doi.org/10.1109/ICICTA.2010.73]

[12]   A. Dwivedi, A. Sharma, and P. S. Mehra, "Energy-aware routing protocols for wireless sensor network based on fuzzy logic: A 10-years analytical review", *EAI Endorsed Trans. Energy Web, Jul.,* 2020.

[13]   J. Li, Z. Huang, and X. Wang, "RETRACTED ARTICLE: Countermeasure research about developing internet of things economy: A case of Hangzhou City", In: *2011 International Conference on E-Business and E-Government, ICEE2011 : Proceedings* IEEE Computer Society, 2011, pp. 8741-8745.

[14]   P. Mehra, M. Doja, and B. Alam, "Stability Enhancement in LEACH (SE-LEACH) for Homogeneous WSN", *ICST Transactions on Scalable Information Systems,* p. 156592, 2018.
[http://dx.doi.org/10.4108/eai.13-7-2018.156592]

[15]   A.K. Bashir, M.S. Park, S. Il Lee, J. Park, W. Lee, and S.C. Shah, In-network RFID data filtering scheme in RFID-WSN for RFID applications.*International Conference on Intelligent Robotics and Applications ICIRA 2013: Intelligent Robotics and Applications,* Springer Link, 2013, pp. 454-465.
[http://dx.doi.org/10.1007/978-3-642-40849-6_46]

[16]   S. Singh, S. Chand, and B. Kumar, "Energy efficient clustering protocol using fuzzy logic for heterogeneous WSNs", *Wirel. Pers. Commun.,* vol. 86, no. 2, pp. 451-475, 2016.
[http://dx.doi.org/10.1007/s11277-015-2939-4]

[17]   O. Rensfelt, F. Hermans, P. Gunningberg, L.A. Larzon, and E. Bjornemo, "Repeatable experiments with mobile nodes in a relocatable WSN testbed", *Comput. J.,* vol. 54, no. 12, pp. 1973-1986, 2011.
[http://dx.doi.org/10.1093/comjnl/bxr052]

[18]   A. Dwivedi, and A. Sharma, "FEECA: Fuzzy based energy efficient clustering approach in wireless sensor network", *ICST Transactions on Scalable Information Systems,* no. Jul, p. 163688, 2018.
[http://dx.doi.org/10.4108/eai.13-7-2018.163688]

[19]   F. Tao, Y. LaiLi, L. Xu, and L. Zhang, "FC-PACO-RM: A parallel method for service composition optimal-selection in a cloud manufacturing system", *IEEE Trans. Industr. Inform.,* vol. 9, no. 4, pp. 2023-2033, 2013.
[http://dx.doi.org/10.1109/TII.2012.2232936]

[20]   P.S. Mehra, M.N. Doja, and B. Alam, *Enhanced Stable Period for Two Level and Multilevel Heterogeneous Model for Distant Base Station in Wireless Sensor Network.* Springer: New Delhi, 2016, pp. 751-759.
[http://dx.doi.org/10.1007/978-81-322-2517-1_72]

[21]   Q. Li, Z. yuan Wang, W. Hua, J. Li, C. Wang, and R. Yang Du, "Applications integration in a hybrid cloud computing environment: Modeling and platform", *Enterprise Inf. Syst.,* vol. 7, no. 3, pp. 237-271, 2013.
[http://dx.doi.org/10.1080/17517575.2012.677479]

[22]   N. Zakaria, and J. A, "Smart city architecture: Vision and challenges", *Int. J. Adv. Comput. Sci. Appl.,* vol. 6, no. 11, 2015.
[http://dx.doi.org/10.14569/IJACSA.2015.061132]

[23]   H.S. Aggarwal, A. Kansal, and A. Jamshed, "Noisy information and progressive data-mining giving rise to privacy preservation", *Proceedings : 2017 3ʳᵈ International Conference on Advances in Computing, Communication and Automation (Fall),* ICACCA 2017, pp. 1–5, 2018.

[24]   S.A. Al-Qaseemi, H.A. Almulhim, M.F. Almulhim, and S.R. Chaudhry, "Internet-of-Things architecture challenges and issues: Lack of standardization", *FTC 2016 : Proceedings of Future*

Technologies Conference, pp. 731-738, 2017.

[25]   A. Jamshed, B. Mallick, and P. Kumar, "Deep learning-based sequential pattern mining for progressive database", *Soft Comput.,* vol. 24, no. 22, pp. 17233-17246, 2020.
[http://dx.doi.org/10.1007/s00500-020-05015-2]

[26]   I.A.T. Hashem, V. Chang, N.B. Anuar, K. Adewole, I. Yaqoob, A. Gani, E. Ahmed, and H. Chiroma, "The role of big data in smart city", *Int. J. Inf. Manage.,* vol. 36, no. 5, pp. 748-758, 2016.
[http://dx.doi.org/10.1016/j.ijinfomgt.2016.05.002]

[27]   A.K. Dwivedi, "EE-LEACH: Energy enhancement in leach to improve network life time of homogeneous wireless sensor network", *Law, State and Telecommunications Review,* vol. 12, no. 1, pp. 205-224, 2020.
[http://dx.doi.org/10.26512/lstr.v12i1.29051]

[28]   L. Catarinucci, D. de Donno, L. Mainetti, L. Palano, L. Patrono, M.L. Stefanizzi, and L. Tarricone, "An IoT-aware architecture for smart healthcare systems", *IEEE Internet Things J.,* vol. 2, no. 6, pp. 515-526, 2015.
[http://dx.doi.org/10.1109/JIOT.2015.2417684]

[29]   A. Dwivedi, A. Sharma, and P. Mehra, "Energy aware routing protocols for wireless sensor network based on fuzzy logic: A 10-years analytical review", *EAI Endorsed Transactions on Energy Web,* no. Jul, p. 166548, 2018.
[http://dx.doi.org/10.4108/eai.6-10-2020.166548]

[30]   S. Chandhok, and R. Anand, "Analysis of sequential mining algorithms", *Int. J. Comp. App.,* vol. 165, no. 12, pp. 14-16, 2017.
[http://dx.doi.org/10.5120/ijca2017914085]

[31]   P. Raj, and A.C. Raman, *The Internet of Things.* Taylor & Francis, CRC Press 2017.: Auerbach Publications: Boca Raton, 2017.

[32]   P.S. Mehra, M.N. Doja, and B. Alam, "Codeword authenticated key exchange (CAKE) light weight secure routing protocol for WSN", *Int. J. Commun. Syst.,* vol. 32, no. 3, p. e3879, 2019.
[http://dx.doi.org/10.1002/dac.3879]

[33]   S. Singh, S. Chand, and B. Kumar, "Multilevel heterogeneous network model for wireless sensor networks", *Telecomm. Syst.,* vol. 64, no. 2, pp. 259-277, 2017.
[http://dx.doi.org/10.1007/s11235-016-0174-2]

[34]   O. Elijah, T.A. Rahman, I. Orikumhi, C.Y. Leow, and M.H.D.N. Hindia, "An overview of internet of things (IoT) and data analytics in agriculture: Benefits and challenges", *IEEE Internet Things J.,* vol. 5, no. 5, pp. 3758-3773, 2018.
[http://dx.doi.org/10.1109/JIOT.2018.2844296]

[35]   A. Zanella, N. Bui, A. Castellani, L. Vangelista, and M. Zorzi, "Internet of things for smart cities", *IEEE Internet Things J.,* vol. 1, no. 1, pp. 22-32, 2014.
[http://dx.doi.org/10.1109/JIOT.2014.2306328]

[36]   F. A. Alaba, M. Othman, I. A. T. Hashem, and F. Alotaibi, "Internet of Things security: A survey", *IEEE Internet Things J.,.* vol. 1, no. 1, pp. 22–32, Feb. 2014.
[http://dx.doi.org/10.1016/j.jnca.2017.04.002]

[37]   P. S. Mehra, M. N. Doja, and B. Alam, "Enhanced stable period for two level and multilevel heterogeneous model for distant base station in wireless sensor network", pp. 751–759, 2016.
[http://dx.doi.org/10.1007/978-81-322-2517-1_72]

[38]   A. Jamshed, "An analysis of trends, developments and transparent issues in the making of indian smart cities", *Smart CitieIntelligent 166042,.* Jul. 2018.
[http://dx.doi.org/10.4108/eai.18-8-2020.166042]

[39]   T.S.J. Darwish, and K. Abu Bakar, "Fog based intelligent transportation big data analytics in the internet of vehicles environment: Motivations, architecture, challenges, and critical issues", *IEEE*

Access, vol. 6, pp. 15679-15701, 2018.
[http://dx.doi.org/10.1109/ACCESS.2018.2815989]

[40]   P. S. Mehra, "E-FUCA: enhancement in unequal fuzzy clustering and routing for sustainable wireless sensor network", *Complex Intell. Syst.,* vol. 8, pp. 393-412, 2021.

[41]   C.L. Wu, L-C. Fu, and L.C. Fu, "Design and realization of a framework for human–system interaction in smart homes", *IEEE Trans. Syst. Man Cybern. A Syst. Hum.,* vol. 42, no. 1, pp. 15-31, 2012.
[http://dx.doi.org/10.1109/TSMCA.2011.2159584]

[42]   C. Bekara, "Security issues and challenges for the internet-of-things-based smart grid", *Procedia Comput. Sci.,* vol. 34, pp. 532-537, 2014.
[http://dx.doi.org/10.1016/j.procs.2014.07.064]

[43]   C.M. Rao, J.R. Babu, S.J. Pimo, A. Dixit, S. Jaiswal, and A. Jamshed, "A comparative study of NLP based semantic web standard model using SPARQL database", *International Conference on Computing Sciences (ICCS),* pp.1-6, 2021.
[http://dx.doi.org/10.1109/ICCS54944.2021.00010]

[44]   P.S. Mehra, M.N. Doja, and B. Alam, "Enhanced clustering algorithm based on fuzzy logic (E-CAFL) for WSN", *Scalable Computing: Practice and Experience,* vol. 20, no. 1, pp. 41-54, 2019.
[http://dx.doi.org/10.12694/scpe.v20i1.1443]

[45]   A. Jamshed, D.P. Kumar, and D.B. Mallick, "Continuous mining approaches with obsolete database: A review", *Int. J. Softw. Comput. Test.,* vol. 4, no. 1, pp. 1-9, 2018.

[46]   H.C.Y. Chan, "Internet of things business models", *J. Serv. Sci. Manag.,* vol. 8, no. 4, pp. 552-568, 2015.
[http://dx.doi.org/10.4236/jssm.2015.84056]

[47]   A. Verma, M. Agrawal, K. Gupta, A. Jamshed, A. Mishra, H. Khatter, G. Gupta, and S.C. Neupane, "Plantosphere: Next generation adaptive and smart agriculture system", *J. Sens.,* vol. 2022, pp. 1-10, 2022.
[http://dx.doi.org/10.1155/2022/5421312]

[48]   D. Asmita, J. Aatif, R. Ravi, K. SRIDHAR, Y. Ajay Reddy, and P N. Renjith, "Enhanced machine learning algorithms lightweight ensemble classification of normal versus leukemic cel", *J. Pharm. Negat. Results,* pp. 496-505, 2022.
[http://dx.doi.org/10.47750/pnr.2022.13.S09.056]

CHAPTER 2

A Perspective View of Bio-Inspire Approaches Employing in Wireless Sensor Networks

Ved Prakash[1,*], Suman Pandey[1] and Deepti Singh[2]

[1] *Department of Computer Science and Engineering, Kamla Nehru Institute of Technology (KNIT), Sultanpur, India*

[2] *Department of Computer Science and Engineering, Netaji Subhas Institute of Technology (NSIT), Delhi, India*

Abstract: In this chapter, we discuss a bio-inspired computational model that utilizes heuristic techniques. This model is robust and possesses optimization capabilities to address obscure and substantiated problems. Swarm intelligence is an integral part of this bio-inspired model, functioning within groups. The nature of these algorithms is non-centralized, drawing inspiration from self-management to solve real-life complex computational problems. Examples include the traveling salesman problem, the shortest path problem, optimal fitness functions, security systems, and the use of optimal computational resources in various areas. The deployment of a Wireless Sensor Network involves a group of sensor nodes, typically implemented at remote locations to observe environmental behaviors. However, these sensor nodes operate on batteries, making replacement or recharge nearly impossible once deployed. Energy is a crucial resource for wireless sensor networks to extend their lifetime. While numerous concepts have been proposed to improve the lifespan of wireless sensor networks, many issues in Wireless Sensor Networks (WSN) are designed as multi-dimensional optimization problems. The bio-inspired model offers a solution to overcome these challenges. Swarm Intelligence proves to be a simple, efficient, and effective computational methodology for addressing various issues in wireless sensor networks, including node localization, clustering, data aggregation, and deployment. The Swarm Intelligence methodology encompasses several algorithms such as Ant Colony Optimization (ACO), Particle Swarm Optimization (PSO), Reactive Search Optimization (RSO), Fish Swarm Algorithm (FSA), Genetic Algorithm (GA), Bacterial Foraging Algorithm (BFA), and Differential Evolution (DE). This chapter introduces Swarm Intelligence-based optimization algorithms and explores the impact of PSO in wireless sensor networks.

Keywords: Ant colony optimization (ACO), Clustering, Fish swarm algorithm (FSA), Particle swarm optimization (PSO), Reactive search optimization (RSO), Swarm intelligence, WSNs.

---

* **Corresponding author Ved Prakash:** Department of Computer Science and Engineering, Kamla Nehru Institute of Technology (KNIT), Sultanpur, India; E-mail: vedprakashknit@gmail.com

Samayveer Singh , Manju, Aruna Malik, and Pradeep Kumar Singh (Eds.)

1. INTRODUCTION

A swarm is a huge group of homogeneous birds, ants, and simple electronic devices (agents) that communicate with each other in their locality and environment without central control to enable an interesting global behavior to emerge. The algorithms depend on a family of population-based and nature-inspired algorithms that have the capability of generating low-cost, high-performance, and stable solutions to multiple difficult issues [1]. Therefore, Swarm Intelligence is an era of artificial intelligence. It identifies activities of social groups in nature as to consider ant colonies, bird flocks, and fish swarms. These agents (insects or swarm folks) are relatively gossamer and have limited capacity on their own [2]. To work together to accomplish the tasks necessary for their survival, they communicate with certain behavioral patterns. Social interactions between individuals can be either direct or indirect. Examples of direct interaction are *via* visual or audio touch, such as honey bees' air dance. Indirect communication occurs when one person changes the situation and the other individuals act in response to the new-fangled (new path) situation, such as ants' pheromone trails that they put down on their way to finding food sources [3]. Fig. **(1)** is the flow chart of process of Swarm Intelligence. In the first step, initialize the positions and velocities of each particle using the random positioning method. In the second step, evaluate the fitness of each particle using objective function. In the third step, check the maximum iteration or optimal position. In the fourth step, if the condition is not satisfied, then update the positions and velocities of particles in the swarm as fitness value and reach the second step, else stop the process. After completion of the process, the final output gives the optimal result. Classical techniques of optimization need a gigantic computational attempt, as problem size incremented complexity of the system increases exponentially. In solving these problems, an optimization technique plays a very important role in moderate space and computational resources and yet producing desirable results, particularly for a single node implementation. The bio-inspired optimization method is alternative to computationally proficient systematic methods. This method of indirect contact is called the technique of stigmergy, meaning communication through the environment. Swarm Intelligence is the subject of the research area discussed in this in-depth article. This paper explores swarm intelligence's most popular model inspired by the pheromone actions of ants to solve the problem of the traveling salesman [4].

Wireless Sensor network is one of the most promising technologies in the field of electro-computer [5] with important various applications for monitoring climate and habitat, structural, health-care, and disaster management [6]. By sensing the physical properties of the environment, a wireless sensor network (WSN) can track the targeted area. WSN is a network of lightweight, cheap self-driving nodes capable of capturing, processing, and transmitting sensory data *via* wireless networks. The final target of the data is one or more base stations (no energy constraints). WSN's technical challenge properties include dense non-infrastructure nodes deployment, dynamic topology, bandwidth, spatial distribution, memory, computing and power resource constraints. There are many factors that also affect WSN, such as deployment, location, EAC (energy-awar--clustering), and data aggregation nodes as problems of optimization. Clustering is one of the most important techniques to improve the lifespan of a Wireless Sensor Network. In this technique, cluster head selection is the most important objective. As per researchers, cluster head selection problem falls in the NP-hard problem for the algorithm. Swarm Intelligence models have the capability to solve NP-hard problems [7]. PSO is a popular technique of multi-dimensional optimization [8]. PSO's strengths are effortless implementation, high-class solutions, software performance, and convergence speed. Literature in WSNs is full of PSO requests. The main target of this is to provide an idea of PSO in WSNs.

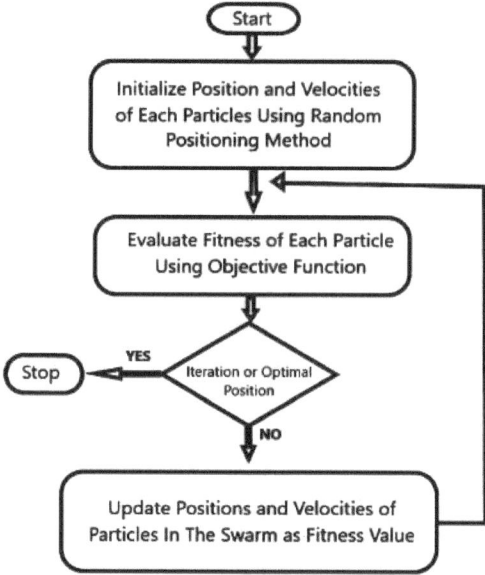

Fig. (1). Process flow diagram of swarm intelligence.

The paper is organized as follows: section 2 discusses the literature review of the related papers. Section 3 discusses the taxonomy of swarm intelligence and the paper is concluded in section 4.

2. LITERATURE SURVEY

Amitabha Ghosh [9] *et al.* examined various fundamental problems related to the wireless sensor network. According to them, the problem domains include sensing coverage and connectivity. In the optimization routine, including node, logic diminished communication overhead, lessened computation, reduced cost, node failure recovery, and also ensured increased coverage with connectivity which can handle challenges in better ways. Quality of service is evaluated in terms of coverage and connectivity in the wireless sensor network, and it also ensures how each point is covered and also ensures information collected by the nodes is accurate. The conclusion is that with constrained resources, better network connectivity and coverage are achieved. Several other studies had been made comparing algorithm and techniques to improve connectivity and coverage.

According to Keisuke [10], in the PSO search technique, a set of agents is utilized that migrates through the search area to get the objective function's minimum value. Each particle's path is defined by a simple relation that involves the research history of a particle, current particle velocity and also the research history of its neighbors. PSO fascinated many researchers due to the reason of high efficient search for a higher-level objective function with many local constructs or optima. The examination of the dynamic particle swarm organization search is done, and further enhancements are suggested. The application to large domain optimization problems and particle swarm optimization research is the highlight of this paper.

Azlina Bt. AbAzi [11] *et al.* indicated that coverage issues in WSN are a matter of concern. Quality of service is directly proportional to coverage rate. A new algorithm is projected, which utilizes PSO and Voronoi diagram to attain better sensor coverage. The purpose of PSO is to get the best deployment of the sensor to attain better coverage, and fitness function is evaluated for the solution using the Voronoi diagram. Results prove better coverage in accordance with better time efficiency.

W. Z. Wan Ismail [12] *et al.*'s paper emphasizes to resolve the coverage issues in WSN by improving the coverage percentage of sensor nodes. PSO algorithm and the effect of sensor nodes in terms of number are studied. The conclusion achieved is that we can enhance the coverage percentage by increasing the number of sensors or by taking a small region of interest. The practicality of the conclusion is not so pleasing because these approaches favor small ROI, and increasing the number of sensor nodes is costly. The coverage problem is handled using PSO, keeping the number of sensor nodes and ROI unaffected.

R. UmaRani [13] *et al.* explained the purpose of this paper is to apply the non-deterministic Ant Colony Algorithm (ACO) in grid computing. Its purpose is to use and share large-scale resources in distributed heterogeneous systems for computation extensive work. A technique for scheduling schemes in grid computing is proposed in this paper. It compares the existing Ant Colony Algorithm (ACO) and the proposed ACO, along with finding the best allocation of resources for the job. This paper presents an enhanced ACO algorithm collaborating concept of the Resource Aware Scheduling Algorithm.

3. TAXONOMY OF SWARM INTELLIGENCE [14]

According to the researchers, Swarm Intelligence can be applied in multidisciplinary models and also be classified into many domains [15]. Fig. (2) shows the taxonomy of the Swarm Intelligence System.

- ACO (Ant colony optimization)
- FSA (Fish Swarm Algorithm)
- PSO (Particle swarm optimization)
- RSO (Reactive Search Optimization)
- Other optimization Algorithms

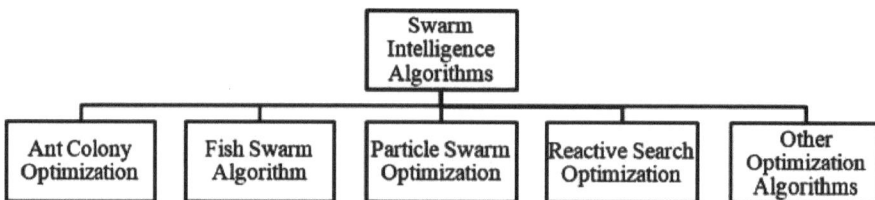

Fig. (2). Taxonomy of swarm intelligence.

3.1. Ant Colony Optimization (ACO)

ACO is a population-based algorithm that can be used to find estimated solutions to difficult problems of optimization. In ACO, a group of computers or devices behave like artificial ants interested in finding the optimal solution to a given problem of optimization. ACO technique applies to find the best route or path on a weighted map. By moving on the map, the artificial bees (hereafter ants) incrementally create solutions. The solution learning process is deterministic and influenced by a pheromone model, *i.e.*, a set of criteria linked with graph components (both nodes and edges) whose values are updated at runtime by the ants [16]. Fig. (3) shows pseudo code for the ant colony optimization technique.

The ACO pseudo code [17]:

```
1.  begin:
2.        initialize
3.        while stopping criterion not satisfied do
4.                position each ant is a starting node
5.                repeat
6.                    for each ant do
7.                            choose next by applying the state transition rule
8.                            Apply step by step pheromone update
9.                    end for
10.               until every ant has built a solution
11.               update best solution
12.               apply offline pheromone update
13.        end while
14.  end
```

Fig. (3). ACO pseudo code.

3.2. Fish Swarm Algorithm (FSA)

It is one of the best approaches to optimize along with Swarm Intelligence optimization approaches. This algorithm is encouraged by the collective activity of the fish and their different social reactions. Based on a series of automatic activities, the fish, for eternity, aim to maintain their colonies and thus exhibit intelligent behaviors. The search for food, emigration, and hazards can all take place in a social process, and conversations between all the fish in a crowd can lead to intelligent social activities. There are many advantages of this algorithm, including quick convergence speed, flexibility, failure resistance, and high precision [18]. Fig. (4) shows pseudo code for the fish swarm algorithm.

The FSA pseudo code [18]:

```
1.  begin:
2.        set t =0;
3.        set initialize P(0);
4.        while (not termination_condition) do
5.                t = t + 1
6.                flag = evaluation P(t);
7.                switch (behavior selection (flag))
8.                        state 1: swarming behavior;
9.                        state 2: following behavior;
10.                       state 3: searching behavior;
11.               bulletin P(t) = P_R + P_N;
12.       end
13.  end
```

Fig. (4). FSA pseudo code.

3.3. Particle Swarm Optimization (PSO)

It is an advanced technique of computation based on the concept of bird flocking. Kennedy and Eberhart proposed this approach for the first time [13]. A set of potential solutions in PSO is called randomly initialized particles. Fig. (5) shows pseudo code for particle swarm optimization technique. Every particle will have a fitness value that will be evaluated for optimization in each generation by the fitness function. Every particle knows its best pBest position and the best position in the whole community of gBest parts so far [19]. While there max iterations or min error criteria are not attained.

The pseudo code of the PSO [20]:

```
1.  for each particle
2.      initialize particle
3.  end
4.  do
5.      for each particle
6.          calculate fitness value
7.          if the fitness value is better than its personal best
8.              set current value as the new pBest
9.      end
10.     choose the particle with the best fitness value of all as gBest
11.     for each particle
12.         calculate particle velocity according equation (a)
13.         update particle position according equation (b)
14.     end
15.  while  maximum iterations or minimum error criteria is not attained
Equation (a)
v[] = c0 * v[] + c1 * rand() * (pBest[] – present[]) + c2 * rand() * (gBest[] – present[])
( in the original method, c0 = 1, but many researchers now play with this parameter)
Equation (b)
present[] = present[] + v[]
```

Fig. (5). PSO pseudo code.

The optimally designed WSN guarantees adequate QoS (service quality) and prolongs the life of the network. On a base station, PSO solutions are centrally measured to evaluate the location of sensors, remote nodes or base stations, as summarized in Table. 1.

Table 1. Role of PSO in different areas for wireless sensor networks.

	Optimization criterion	Algorithm	Centralized	Distributed	Data fusion	SCH	Placement
1.	Max. coverage	PSO_Voronoi [21]	χ	√	√	√	χ
2.	Max. energy efficiency	PSO multi-base [22]	χ	χ	√	√	χ
3.	Min. cost of sensor equipment	Pso_traffic [23]	χ	√	√	√	χ
4.	Prolong network	Pso_c [24]	χ	√	√	χ	√
5.	Prolong network	MSTree-PSO [25]	χ	√	√	χ	√

(Table 1) cont.....

	Optimization criterion	Algorithm	Centralized	Distributed	Data fusion	SCH	Placement
6.	Reduce intra-cluster distance	PSO_clustering [26]	χ	√	√	χ	√
7.	Min. decision error and transaction time	BMPSO [27]	√	χ	χ	√	√
8.	Min. decision error	ABC_PSO [28]	χ	√	χ	√	√
9.	Min. energy expenditure and error probability	PSO_Opt_Alloc [29]	χ	√	χ	√	√

χ = Yes and √ = No

3.4. Reactive Search Optimization (RSO)

Emphasizes the application of machine learning methods to seek out heuristics to solve difficult and complex problems of optimization. The declaration reactive implies a ready reaction to the incident while exploring alternative approaches for essential factor self-tuning by means of an internal virtual feedback loop. Fig. (6) shows pseudo code for the reactive search optimization technique. The power lies in integrating sophisticated skills that are often related to the nervous system, such as learning from previous experiences, learning at work, fast investigation of alternatives, ability to handle inaccurate information, and rapid adjustment to novel conditions and events [30].

The RSO pseudo code [30]:

```
1.  function Variable_Neighborhood_Descent(N₁,N₂, ........,Nₖₘₐₓ)
2.         repeat until no improvement or max CPU time elapsed
3.               k←1 // index of default neighborhood exploration
4.               while k ≤ kₘₐₓ:
5.                     X' ← BestNeighbor(Nₖ(X)) //neighborhood exploration
6.                     if f(X')<f(X)
7.                        X ← X'; k ← 1 // success back to default neighborhood
8.                     else
9.                        k ← k + 1 // try with the following neighborhood
10. end
```

Fig. (6). RSO pseudo code.

The Variable_Neighborhood_Descent routine: Neighborhoods with higher numbers are considered only if the default neighborhood fails and only until an improving move is identified. X is the current point.

3.5. Other Optimization Algorithms

Common approaches to optimization include 1. Linear, 2. Nonlinear, 3. Quadratic programming, Newton-based techniques, and methods of an internal point. Computational complexities are increasing exponentially due to the problem dimension [31]. The resource requirements and costs of computer programming engines used for linear, nonlinear and quadratic programming (such as IBM ILOG CPLEX) allow them Space-restricted nodes that are undesirable [32]. Heuristic algorithms such as PSO, GA, Differential- Evolution (DE) and Bacterial-Forestr--Algorithm (BFA) inspire this. GA promotes population growth using 1. Crossover, 2. Mutation and 3. Selection methods [11], generation by generation. DE is the same as GA, but a differential form is used [12]. This produces a fresh vector solution by randomly selected mutation of the original vector. BFA models the bacteria's foraging activities by mixing straight and arbitrary motions for nutrient-friendly exposure to locations [13]. The following are PSO's advantages over these alternatives:

1) It can be easily implemented on both hardware and software.

2) Selection parameters available.

3) High-quality solutions because of their ability to escape from local optima.

4) Variants are available for real integer and binary domains.

5) Fast convergence.

Table 2 describes the impact of the particle swarm optimization algorithm on the WSN in various problems in previous years. As per research, the nature of wireless sensor networks is decentralized with low communication bandwidth and limited battery energy, and is implemented in remote locations and faces the problem of a lifetime of the network. Particle swarm optimization algorithm has the capacity to track such types of optimization issues very efficiently and effectively.

Table 2. Impact of PSO on WSN.

Ref.	Year	Optimize Routing	Optimize Scalability	Energy Efficient	Optimize Lifetime	Optimize Node Localization	Optimize Latency	Cluster Based	Grid Based	Other Type of Network	Mobility of Node	Data Aggregation	Optimize Communication	Robust Network	Coverage	Multi objective	Security
[33]	2020	χ	χ	χ	χ	√	√	χ	√	√	√	χ	χ	χ	√	√	√
[34]	2020	√	√	√	√	√	√	χ	√	√	√	χ	χ	√	√	√	χ
[35]	2020	√	χ	√	χ	χ	χ	√	√	χ	√	χ	χ	√	√	√	χ
[36]	2020	√	√	χ	√	χ	√	√	√	χ	χ	√	χ	χ	√	√	√
[37]	2019	√	χ	√	χ	χ	√	√	√	χ	√	√	χ	√	χ	√	√
[38]	2019	χ	χ	χ	χ	χ	√	χ	√	√	√	χ	χ	√	√	√	√
[39]	2019	χ	√	χ	χ	√	χ	χ	√	√	χ	χ	χ	√	√	√	√
[40]	2019	√	√	χ	χ	√	√	χ	√	√	√	χ	χ	√	√	√	√

(Table 2) cont.....

Ref.	Year	Optimize Routing	Optimize Scalability	Energy Efficient	Optimize Lifetime	Optimize Node Localization	Optimize Latency	Cluster Based	Grid Based	Other Type of Network	Mobility of Node	Data Aggregation	Optimize Communication	Robust Network	Coverage	Multi objective	Security
[41]	2019	χ	√	χ	χ	√	χ	χ	√	√	χ	√	χ	√	√	√	√
[42]	2018	χ	χ	χ	χ	√	√	χ	√	√	√	χ	χ	√	√	√	√
[43]	2018	√	√	χ	χ	√	√	√	√	√	√	√	√	χ	√	χ	√
[44]	2018	√	√	χ	χ	√	√	χ	√	√	√	χ	χ	√	√	√	√
[45]	2018	√	√	χ	χ	√	√	χ	√	√	√	χ	χ	√	√	√	√
[46]	2018	√	√	χ	χ	χ	√	√	χ	√	√	χ	χ	√	√	√	√
[47]	2018	√	χ	χ	χ	√	√	√	χ	√	√	√		√	χ	√	√
[48]	2018	√	√	χ	χ	√	√	χ	√	√	√	√	χ	√	√	√	√
[49]	2016	χ	√	χ	χ	√	χ	χ	√	√	√	χ	χ	√	√	√	√
[50]	2016	χ	χ	χ	χ	χ	√	χ	√	√	√	χ	χ	√	√	χ	√
[51]	2013	√	χ	χ	χ	χ	√	χ	√	√	χ	χ	χ	χ	√	√	√
[52]	2013	√	√		χ	χ	√	√	χ	√	√	χ	χ	χ	√	√	√
[53]	2011	χ	√	χ	χ	χ	√	χ	√	√	√	χ	χ	√	√	√	√
[54]	2011	√	√	χ	χ	χ	√	χ	χ	√	√	χ	χ	√	√	χ	√

χ = Yes and √ = No

CONCLUSION

The main concepts and principles of bio-inspired are completely based on the natural behaviour of the swarm intelligence system and insects. The swarm intelligence model contains many optimization algorithms such as Ant Colony Optimization, Fish Swarm Algorithm, Particle Swarm Optimization, Reactive Search Optimization, and other optimization algorithms. Substance and scale of deployment, surroundings uncertainties and energy limitation, bandwidth, space, and resources of computing are significant challenges to WSNs developers. WSNs issues of localization, clustering of energy awareness, node deployment, and data aggregation are frequently formulated as problems of optimization. Most analytical methods suffer from slowness or lack of convergence with the final solutions. This requires fast optimization algorithms that produce quality solutions using fewer resources. PSO is a popular technique used to solve optimization problems in WSN due to its ease, high quality of the solution, rapid convergence and negligible computational load. However, the iterative nature of PSO may prohibit its use for high-speed real-time applications, especially if optimization is performed frequently.

REFERENCES

[1] Preeti Sethi, "Swarm intelligence for clustering in wireless sensor networks", *Swarm Intelligence Optimization: Algorithms and Applications,* pp. 263-273, 2020.
[http://dx.doi.org/10.1002/9781119778868.ch13]

[2] Zhihua Cui, and Xiaozhi Gao, "Theory and applications of swarm intelligence", pp. 205-206, 2012.
[http://dx.doi.org/10.1007/s00521-011-0523-8]

[3] A. Nayyar, and R. Singh, "Ant colony optimization computational swarm intelligence technique", . *2016 3rd International conference on computing for sustainable global development (INDIACom), IEEE,* 2016.

[4] Hazem Ahmed, and Janice Glasgow, *Swarm intelligence: Concepts, models and applications.* School of Computing, Queens University Technical Report, 2012.

[5]   Mohammad Abdul Matin, and M. M. Islam, "Overview of wireless sensor network", *Wireless sensor networks-technology and protocols,* pp. 1-3, 2012.
[http://dx.doi.org/10.5772/49376]

[6]   V. Prakash, S. Pandey, and A.K. Singh, "Basic introduction of wireless sensor network", *Proceedings of 2nd International Conference on Advanced Computing and Software Engineering (ICACSE),* 2019.

[7]   Weifeng Sun, "A survey of using swarm intelligence algorithms in IoT", *Sensors 20.5.* 1420, 2020.
[http://dx.doi.org/10.3390/s20051420]

[8]   W.A. Hammood, K.Z. Zamil, and A.M. Ali, "A Review of bio-inspired algorithm", *Conference:(SOFTEC Asia 2017), at Kuala Lumpur Convention Centre.* Vol. 12. 2017.

[9]   A. Ghosh, and S.K. Das, "Coverage and connectivity issues in wireless sensor networks: A survey", *Pervasive Mobile Comput.,* vol. 4, no. 3, pp. 303-334, 2008.
[http://dx.doi.org/10.1016/j.pmcj.2008.02.001]

[10]   K. Kameyama, "Particle swarm optimization : A survey", *IEICE Trans. Inf. Syst.,* vol. E92-D, no. 7, pp. 1354-1361, 2009.
[http://dx.doi.org/10.1587/transinf.E92.D.1354]

[11]   A. Aziz, and N. Azlina, "Wireless sensor networks coverage-energy algorithms based on particle swarm optimization", *Emir. J. Eng. Res.,* vol. 18, no. 2, pp. 41-52, 2013.

[12]   W.Z. Ismail, and S. Abd Manaf, "Study on coverage in wireless sensor network using grid based strategy and particle swarm optimization", *2010 IEEE Asia Pacific Conference on Circuits and Systems,* 2010.
[http://dx.doi.org/10.1109/APCCAS.2010.5775080]

[13]   D. Palupi Rini, S. Mariyam Shamsuddin, and S. Sophiyati Yuhaniz, "Particle swarm optimization: Technique, system and challenges", *Int. J. Comput. Appl.,* vol. 14, no. 1, pp. 19-27, 2011.
[http://dx.doi.org/10.5120/1810-2331]

[14]   Lucija Brezočnik, Iztok Fister, and Vili Podgorelec, "Swarm intelligence algorithms for feature selection: A review", *Appl. Sci..* 1521, 2018.
[http://dx.doi.org/10.3390/app8091521]

[15]   Y. Cai, and A. Sharma, "Swarm intelligence optimization: An exploration and application of machine learning technology", *J. Intell. Syst.,* vol. 30, no. 1, pp. 460-469, 2021.
[http://dx.doi.org/10.1515/jisys-2020-0084]

[16]   S. Mirjalili, *Ant colony optimisation.* Springer: Cham, 2019, pp. 33-42.
[http://dx.doi.org/10.1007/978-3-319-93025-1_3]

[17]   D.N. Kumar, and M.J. Reddy, "Ant colony optimization for multi-purpose reservoir operation", *Water Resour. Manage.,* vol. 20, no. 6, pp. 879-898, 2006.
[http://dx.doi.org/10.1007/s11269-005-9012-0]

[18]   M. Neshat, "A review of artificial fish swarm optimization methods and applications", *Int. J. Smart Sensing Intell. Syst.,* vol. 5, p. 1, 2017.

[19]   B. Pitchaimanickam, and S. Radhakrishnan, "A hybrid bacteria foraging using particle swarm optimization algorithm for clustering in wireless sensor networks", *2014 International Conference on Science Engineering and Management Research (ICSEMR),* 2014.
[http://dx.doi.org/10.1109/ICSEMR.2014.7043588]

[20]   Available from: http://www.swarmintelligence.org/tutorials.php

[21]   A. Aziz, N.A. Bt, A.W. Mohemmed, and B.S. Daya Sagar, "Particle swarm optimization and Voronoi diagram for wireless sensor networks coverage optimization", *2007 International Conference on Intelligent and Advanced Systems,* 2007.
[http://dx.doi.org/10.1109/ICIAS.2007.4658528]

[22]   Z-J. Teng, "Particle swarm optimization algorithm based on dynamic acceleration factor in wireless sensor network", *J. Inf. Hiding Multim. Signal Process.*, vol. 9, no. 5, pp. 1245-1254, 2018.

[23]   J. Hu, J. Song, M. Zhang, and X. Kang, "Topology optimization for urban traffic sensor network", *Tsinghua Sci. Technol.*, vol. 13, no. 2, pp. 229-236, 2008.
[http://dx.doi.org/10.1016/S1007-0214(08)70037-3]

[24]   N.M. Latiff, "Energy-aware clustering for wireless sensor networks using particle swarm optimization", *2007 IEEE 18th international symposium on personal, indoor and mobile radio communications. IEEE*, 2007.

[25]   X. Cao, "Cluster heads election analysis for multi-hop wireless sensor networks based on weighted graph and particle swarm optimization", *2008 Fourth International Conference on Natural Computation*, vol. 7, 2008.
[http://dx.doi.org/10.1109/ICNC.2008.693]

[26]   S.M. Guru, S.K. Halgamuge, and S. Fernando, "Particle swarm optimisers for cluster formation in wireless sensor networks", *2005 International Conference on Intelligent Sensors, Sensor Networks and Information Processing*, IEEE, 2005.
[http://dx.doi.org/10.1109/ISSNIP.2005.1595599]

[27]   K.K. Veeramachaneni, and L.A. Osadciw, "Dynamic sensor management using multi-objective particle swarm optimizer", *Multisensor, Multisource Information Fusion: Architectures, Algorithms, and Applications 2004. International Society for Optics and Photonics*, vol. 5434, 2004.

[28]   K. Veeramachaneni, and L. Osadciw, "Swarm intelligence based optimization and control of decentralized serial sensor networks", *2008 IEEE Swarm Intelligence Symposium*, IEEE, 2008.
[http://dx.doi.org/10.1109/SIS.2008.4668332]

[29]   T. Wimalajeewa, and S.K. Jayaweera, "Optimal power scheduling for correlated data fusion in wireless sensor networks via constrained PSO", *IEEE Trans. Wirel. Commun.*, vol. 7, no. 9, pp. 3608-3618, 2008.
[http://dx.doi.org/10.1109/TWC.2008.070386]

[30]   R. Battiti, and M. Brunato, Reactive search optimization: learning while optimizing. *Handbook of Metaheuristics.* Springer: Boston, MA, 2010, pp. 543-571.
[http://dx.doi.org/10.1007/978-1-4419-1665-5_18]

[31]   M.T.M. Emmerich, and A.H. Deutz, "A tutorial on multiobjective optimization: Fundamentals and evolutionary methods", *Nat. Comput.*, vol. 17, no. 3, pp. 585-609, 2018.
[http://dx.doi.org/10.1007/s11047-018-9685-y] [PMID: 30174562]

[32]   C. Bliek1ú, B. Pierre, and L. Andrea, "Solving mixed-integer quadratic programming problems with IBM-CPLEX: A progress report", *Proceedings of the twenty-sixth RAMP symposium*, 2014.

[33]   A. Kaushik, M. Goswami, M. Manuja, S. Indu, and D. Gupta, "A binary PSO approach for improving the performance of wireless sensor networks", *Wirel. Pers. Commun.*, vol. 113, no. 1, pp. 263-297, 2020.
[http://dx.doi.org/10.1007/s11277-020-07188-3]

[34]   J. Yuan, "An anomaly data mining method for mass sensor networks using improved PSO algorithm based on spark parallel framework", *J. Grid Comput.*, vol. 18, no. 2, pp. 251-261, 2020.
[http://dx.doi.org/10.1007/s10723-020-09505-3]

[35]   Ying Zhang, Guangyuan Yang, and Bin Zhang, "FW-PSO algorithm to enhance the invulnerability of industrial wireless sensor networks topology", *Sensors*, p. 1114, 2020.
[http://dx.doi.org/10.3390/s20041114]

[36]   Y. Lv, W. Liu, Z. Wang, and Z. Zhang, "WSN localization technology based on hybrid GA-PSO-BP algorithm for indoor three-dimensional space", *Wirel. Pers. Commun.*, vol. 114, no. 1, pp. 167-184, 2020.
[http://dx.doi.org/10.1007/s11277-020-07357-4]

[37] D. Xue, "Research on range-free location algorithm for wireless sensor network based on particle swarm optimization", *EURASIP J. Wirel. Commun. Netw.,* vol. 2019, no. 1, p. 221, 2019.
[http://dx.doi.org/10.1186/s13638-019-1540-z]

[38] S. Prithi, and S. Sumathi, "LD2FA-PSO: A novel Learning Dynamic Deterministic Finite Automata with PSO algorithm for secured energy efficient routing in Wireless Sensor Network", *Ad Hoc Netw.,* vol. 97, p. 102024, 2020.
[http://dx.doi.org/10.1016/j.adhoc.2019.102024]

[39] Jin Wang, "An improved routing schema with special clustering using PSO algorithm for heterogeneous wireless sensor network", *Ad Hoc Networks.* 97 (2020): 102024.
[http://dx.doi.org/10.3390/s19030671]

[40] S.P. Singh, and S.C. Sharma, "Implementation of a PSO based improved localization algorithm for wireless sensor networks", *J. Inst. Electron. Telecommun. Eng.,* vol. 65, no. 4, pp. 502-514, 2019.
[http://dx.doi.org/10.1080/03772063.2018.1436472]

[41] S. Tabibi, and A. Ghaffari, "Energy-efficient routing mechanism for mobile sink in wireless sensor networks using particle swarm optimization algorithm", *Wirel. Pers. Commun.,* vol. 104, no. 1, pp. 199-216, 2019.
[http://dx.doi.org/10.1007/s11277-018-6015-8]

[42] A. Agnihotri, and I.K. Gupta, "A hybrid PSO-GA algorithm for routing in wireless sensor network", *2018 4th International Conference on Recent Advances in Information Technology (RAIT), IEEE,* 2018.
[http://dx.doi.org/10.1109/RAIT.2018.8389082]

[43] Mohammed A. El-Shorbagy, "A novel PSO algorithm for dynamic wireless sensor network multiobjective optimization problem", *Transactions on Emerging Telecommunications Technologies,* 2019.
[http://dx.doi.org/10.1002/ett.3523]

[44] Pradeep Kanchan, and Shetty D. Pushparaj, "A quantum inspired PSO algorithm for energy efficient clustering in wireless sensor networks", *Cogent Engineering 5.1.* (2018): 1522086.
[http://dx.doi.org/10.1080/23311916.2018.1522086]

[45] A. Yadav, S. Kumar, and S. Vijendra, "Network life time analysis of WSNs using particle swarm optimization", *Procedia Comput. Sci.,* vol. 132, pp. 805-815, 2018.
[http://dx.doi.org/10.1016/j.procs.2018.05.092]

[46] M.S. Pramod, "Implementation of hybrid routing protocols in wireless sensor networks", *2018 3rd IEEE International Conference on Recent Trends in Electronics, Information & Communication Technology (RTEICT), IEEE,* 2018.
[http://dx.doi.org/10.1109/RTEICT42901.2018.9012252]

[47] Supreet Kaur, and Rajiv Mahajan, "Hybrid meta-heuristic optimization based energy efficient protocol for wireless sensor networks", *Egyptian Inform. J..* 19.3 (2018): 145-150.
[http://dx.doi.org/10.1016/j.eij.2018.01.002]

[48] R.C. Herakal, and S. Talanki, "Simulation of AI based PSO algorithm in WSN", *IACSIT Int. J. Eng. Technol.,* vol. 7, no. 4, pp. 5132-5136, 2018.

[49] C. Vimalarani, R. Subramanian, and S.N. Sivanandam, "An enhanced PSO-based clustering energy optimization algorithm for wireless sensor network", *Scient.Wor.J.,* vol. 2016, pp. 1-11, 2016.
[http://dx.doi.org/10.1155/2016/8658760] [PMID: 26881273]

[50] M. Azharuddin, and P.K. Jana, "PSO-based approach for energy-efficient and energy-balanced routing and clustering in wireless sensor networks", *Soft Comput.,* vol. 21, no. 22, pp. 6825-6839, 2017.
[http://dx.doi.org/10.1007/s00500-016-2234-7]

[51] S.M.M. Islam, A.R.R. Mohammad, and M.A. Kiber, "Wireless sensor network using particle swarm optimization", *Proc. of Int. Conf. on Advances in Control System and Electricals Engineering,* 2013.

[52]   B. Gaur, and P. Kumar, "Wireless sensor deployment using modified discrete binary PSO method", *Int. J. Innov. Res. Elect. Electro. Instrumen. Cont. Eng.,* vol. 1, no. 3, pp. 82-89, 2013.

[53]   H. Yu, and W. Xiaohui, "PSO-based energy-balanced double cluster-heads clustering routing for wireless sensor networks", *Procedia Eng.,* vol. 15, pp. 3073-3077, 2011.
       [http://dx.doi.org/10.1016/j.proeng.2011.08.576]

[54]   S. Hojjatoleslami, V. Aghazarian, and A. Aliabadi, "DE based node placement optimization for wireless sensor networks", *2011 3rd International Workshop on Intelligent Systems and Applications, IEEE,* 2011.
       [http://dx.doi.org/10.1109/ISA.2011.5873254]

CHAPTER 3

Automatic Accident Detection and Alerting System using IoT

Aman Jatain[1,*], Sarika Chaudhary[2] and Manju[3]

[1] *Department of Computer Science and Engineering, Amity University, Haryana, India*

[2] *Manav Rachna International Institute of Research and Studies (MRIIRS), Faridabad, Mohali, India*

[3] *Department of Computer Science and Information Technology, Jaypee Institute of Information Technology, Noida, Uttar Pradesh, India*

Abstract: This chapter proposes the implementation of an automatic accident detection and alerting system utilizing the Internet of Things (IoT). This system aims to swiftly and efficiently locate accident sites and notify emergency services, there by expediting the transfer of victims to medical centers. Road accidents are one of the leading causes of death annually, primarily due to delays in reporting the incidents. The proposed system operates in two main parts. First, when a vehicle is impacted, sensors installed in the vehicle activate and capture the location *via* the Global System for Mobile Communication (GSM) module. Subsequently, information about the accident site and the victim's condition is sent to a registered phone number through the GSM module. Essentially, when an accident occurs, the installed piezoelectric sensor immediately detects the impact, relaying this information to the microcontroller. The microcontroller then sends an alert message, including location and other pertinent details, to the registered unit to ensure timely medical assistance. This system aims to enhance the efficiency of medical services in reaching accident victims promptly, potentially saving lives that might otherwise be lost due to delayed accident reporting.

Keywords: Automatic accident detection, Alerting system, GSM, General packet radio service (GPRS), Internet of things vehicle, LTE.

1. INTRODUCTION

Road accidents are a leading cause of mortality worldwide, posing a significant global health challenge. The annual death toll from road traffic incidents is alarmingly high, underscoring a crisis in road safety [1]. Each year, road accidents claim the lives of 1.3 million people and injure approximately 50 million more worldwide. On average, this translates to 3,287 lives lost daily.

* **Corresponding author Aman Jatain:** Department of Computer Science and Engineering, Amity University, Haryana, India; E-mail: amanjatainsingh@gmail.com

Samayveer Singh , Manju, Aruna Malik, and Pradeep Kumar Singh (Eds.)

Notably, road traffic deaths disproportionately affect young adults, accounting for more than 50% of fatalities. In particular, around 40,000 individuals aged 25 and below lose their lives in road accidents annually [2]. This dire situation is not confined to specific countries; even nations with robust road safety measures experience a significant number of fatalities each year due to road traffic incidents. In India, the statistics are particularly alarming. In year 2013 there were 1.3 lakh casualties from road accidents, a figure surpassing the total number of casualties from all wars combined [3]. Furthermore, in 2017, road accidents resulted in 1.46 lakh fatalities, a number equivalent to the entire population of Shillong, the capital of Meghalaya. Annually, road accidents claim over a lakh lives in India, and the ratio of injuries to fatalities is approximately three to four times higher [4].

There could be many possible reasons for deaths in road accidents, but these should be examined because the world we live in is based on technology, and we cannot ever deny the fact that everyone in this era is a slave to technology. Technology has made our lives easier in many ways. However, with the advancement in technology, everyone is looking for an easy life, and this desire for technology affects every individual. For example, the excessive use of automobiles has increased the occurrence of traffic hazards and road accidents. The very reason for a person's demise in a road accident is often the delay in the process of conveying this information to medical centers [3]. Something extremely essential for the victims of vehicle accidents is emergency response time; when it comes to life, every minute counts. This applies to both the present and the future. Despite so much advancement in technology, there is still a lack of providing emergency services on time. From an analytical viewpoint, a just one-minute reduction in response time can increase a person's odds of survival by 6%. If an accident occurs, someone will have to inform the police or hospital personnel about the accident; then help will arrive, and it is also unknown how much time this process will take. Due to poor traffic management and delays in the transfer of accident information, it is impossible to be on time. However, with so much advancement in technology, a system can be designed to help manage traffic and accidents occurring on roads.

Vehicles equipped with advanced safety measures for accident avoidance represent an emerging concept that can be realized through technologies such as IoT, machine learning, and several others. These technologies can be utilized to construct a system that significantly contributes to mitigating road hazards. It is crucial to implement such advanced technologies in traffic and vehicles to reduce response times. In literature, extensive research has been conducted on accident rescue, predominantly focusing on the use of Information and Communication Technology (ICT) for efficient and rapid rescue operations. However, the majority of these works propose sophisticated solutions aimed at decreasing response times. While these solutions are comprehensive, they tend to be expensive and are not universally accessible to all vehicle types. Bearing this in mind, this research aims to introduce the design and implementation of an automatic accident detection system capable of autonomously capturing accident information and location, subsequently transmitting it to a corresponding unit. This functionality is instrumental in reducing the time required to communicate the occurrence of an accident, ultimately expediting the arrival of medical assistance to the accident site [5]. The system proposed herein autonomously detects accidents and proficiently locates the geographical position of the accident site. An Arduino microcontroller, selected for its cost-effectiveness and efficiency, powers the system. Programming is conducted using the Arduino IDE, and various modules are employed for tracking and detection purposes. The system is designed to rapidly detect accidents and promptly convey essential information to the relevant unit, including the accident site's latitude and longitude. Messages are transmitted swiftly, aiding in the preservation of precious lives. A button is incorporated to cease message transmission in rare instances where there are no casualties, ensuring the rescue team's time is not wasted. Upon the occurrence of an accident, the system automatically activates and dispatches an alert message. This message is transmitted *via* GSM/LTE, a mobile communication technology that facilitates the exchange of mobile voice and data services. For communication between the mobile station and the Base Transceiver Station, the system operates within the 890MHz to 915MHz range for one direction, and 935MHz to 960MHz for the other [6]. The GPS module ascertains the accident location's coordinates, while various other sensors are integrated into the proposed system.

As this system is automatic, capable of detecting accidents, and even able to ascertain the critical state of a patient, consider the potential impact if it were installed in every vehicle. This capability would streamline the process of understanding the actual critical state of a victim involved in an accident, enabling medical centers to dispatch help that is appropriately tailored to the situation. This feature enhances the value and utility of the design considerably. To further support rescue teams and minimize their efforts in cases of minor accidents, several additional features have been integrated. An emergency button is included, allowing individuals involved in an accident to communicate that the situation is not dire, obviating the need for extensive rescue efforts. Additionally, a heat sensor is incorporated to detect the onset of a fire, providing an early warning and potentially averting a more serious disaster. Overall, this system offers a comprehensive solution to the inadequate emergency facilities often available for road accidents, addressing the issue in the most effective manner possible.

2. RELATED WORK

This chapter aims to bridge the gap between the current state of research and publications in the field of road safety projects, elucidating the methodologies employed to surmount the limitations inherent in traditional systems. Numerous models and systems have been proposed earlier, offering solutions to road hazards and striving to preserve the precious lives lost in staggering numbers to road accidents. Fig. (**1**) delineates the sequence of events in the accident detection system. Various systems have been suggested by researchers, incorporating technologies such as smartphones, GSM and GPS, vehicular ad-hoc networks, and mobile applications to detect accidents. The technologies employed in these models are state-of-the-art and highly efficient, ranging from smartphones and Intelligent Transportation Systems (ITS) technology to the Internet of Things (IoT). Moreover, the hardware utilized in these models is both cost-effective and proficient.

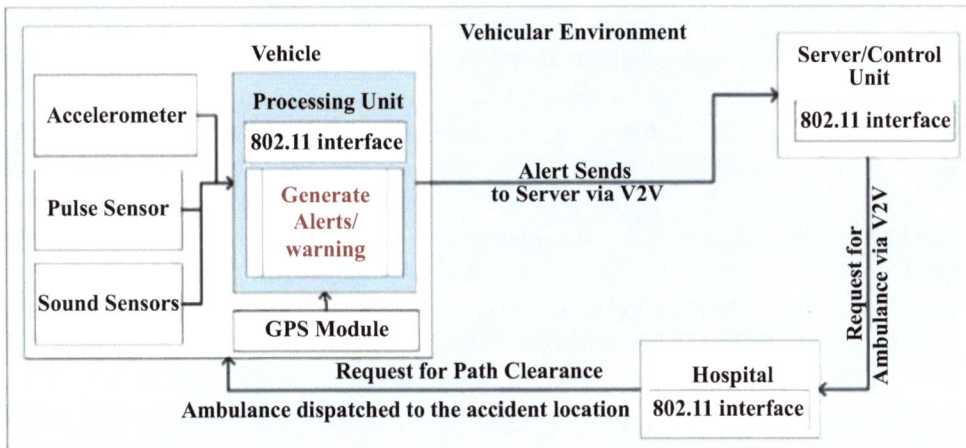

Fig. (1). Flow of accident detection.

Gel *et al.* [1] introduced a system adept at identifying accidents and alerting nearby emergency centers by pinpointing the location using diverse sensors. This research delves into the implementation of hardware components alongside an application designed to transmit information about the accident, ensuring timely assistance to the victim. The system leverages IoT and various hardware components, including ultrasonic sensors, accelerometers, and Arduino, among others. To transmit signals, an ultrasonic sensor is connected to an Arduino UNO board. The ultrasonic sensor emits high-frequency sound waves at regular intervals. An accelerometer is also employed to detect any abrupt changes in the vehicle's axes; it functions efficiently by sending a signal to the Arduino UNO when the vehicle's speed surpasses a predetermined threshold. Additionally, a U-slot positional sensor is used to ascertain the wheel's position. Upon detecting any deviation from the vehicle's normal state, the module sends signals, along with the car's location, to the Arduino UNO. The Arduino UNO subsequently communicates with the GPRS to track the location, facilitating the rapid transmission of this crucial data to nearby medical centers.

James *et al.* [7] developed a security method aimed at curbing automobile theft by introducing an auto theft prevention module, which includes several enhancements such as a fingerprint module, passcode system, and one-time-passcode (OTP) generating mechanism. This research incorporates the use of a fingerprint recognition module, GPS receiver, and GSM module for its advancements. In addition, a module for accident detection has been integrated with these components. To facilitate the timely arrival of an ambulance to the needed location, the driver receives directions from an Android application. The primary objectives of this project are the automatic detection of accidents and the expedited dispatch of an ambulance, complete with necessary guidance. The work promises to deliver a robust security method for preventing vehicle theft while simultaneously addressing accident detection. In the automobile industry today, there is a paramount need for effective security measures and theft prevention. However, reflecting on past practices reveals that a key fob has predominantly been used to arm and disarm modern automobiles. To address these lax security measures and provide more robust protection, this project employs fingerprint recognition alongside a passcode keypad and a one-time passcode-generating system, thereby authorizing vehicle startup. A PIC microcontroller is utilized to manage these operations. The working flow encompasses the identification of the owner's fingerprint by the fingerprint recognition module, which acts as the passcode required to start the engine. The fingerprint module has been pre-trained with various sets of the owner's fingerprints, ensuring efficient and accurate identification. If a fingerprint mismatch occurs, authorization is denied. In addition to fingerprint authorization, the system also incorporates a passcode and OTP generating mechanism. A keypad is provided for inputting and resetting the passcode. The owner gains authorization by entering the correct passcode and has the option to change it after inputting the previous one. Upon successful passcode entry, the OTP generating system activates, providing a temporary passcode for vehicle access. The user must then enter this OTP *via* the keypad. A mismatch results in an 'unauthorized access' message displayed on the LCD, whereas a match turns on the vehicle relay, granting access to the vehicle. Upon engine startup, a message is sent to the owner *via* GSM. In the event of a vehicle hijacking, the owner can immobilize the vehicle by sending an 'OFF' message. This proposed system also includes an accident detection module to ensure rapid and effective assistance for injured individuals. The project integrates various remotely organized devices with the microcontroller, and the ambulance driver, aided by the Android application, can promptly reach the required location. The ultimate goal of this project is to automate accident detection and facilitate the guided dispatch of an ambulance.

Khaliq *et al.* [8] implemented a system complemented by a prototype to offer a solution for managing traffic and ensuring the safety of individuals involved in road accidents, utilizing the integration of two technologies: Vehicular Ad Hoc Networks (VANET) and the Internet of Things (IoT). The system module operates in such a manner that it detects accidents and promptly sends an informative message to the control room, aiming to facilitate the provision of the nearest possible assistance. In this project, the authors developed a TestBed and a prototype deemed efficient enough to identify the occurrence of an accident and to communicate this information automatically to emergency centers, utilizing various sensors and modules embedded in the vehicle. A significant aspect of this project involves the implementation of hardware designed to detect any impact on the vehicle, based on four different modules. These modules operate independently yet are synchronized by devices relying on either VANET or IoT technologies. The primary objective of this project is to expedite the provision of medical assistance to accident victims through the use of these modules. For accident detection, various electromechanical and biomedical sensors are utilized, working in tandem to detect the accident and subsequently communicate the necessary information to medical centers. The proposed system is designed to be functional in environments supported by both VANET and IoT.

Fernandes *et al.* [9] employ the Intelligent Transportation System (ITS) and eCall technology—ITS being a comprehensive framework aimed at making transportation safer and more efficient. Fig. (**2**) illustrates the various components of the system proposed by Fernandes *et al.* With the swift progression of technology, opportunities for global implementation of such systems to mitigate road hazards and reduce traffic accident occurrences have emerged. Acknowledging this, the European Union has initiated the eCallfacility, striving to promptly assist those who previously may have lost their lives due to delayed medical response. This particular research introduces the HDycopilot, an application designed for accident detection that integrates with multimodal eCall circulation *via* eCall. The system utilizes smartphone sensors, such as an accelerometer and a magnetometer, and receives input directly from the vehicle through these sensors. In the event of a crash, the system is engineered to automatically request assistance from Emergency Medical Services (EMS) through the European helpline emergency number *via* oneCall. Implementing this eCallsystem requires the enforcement of several technologies throughout the chain, involving three primary entities: car manufacturers, mobile network operators, and participating countries. Within this system, if a vehicle experiences a crash, the Android module embedded in the vehicle will initiate an eCall, connecting with the public safety answering point *via* the mobile network operators. In addition, several protocols are utilized for the transmission and reception of messages necessary to alert authorities and seek assistance for the victims.

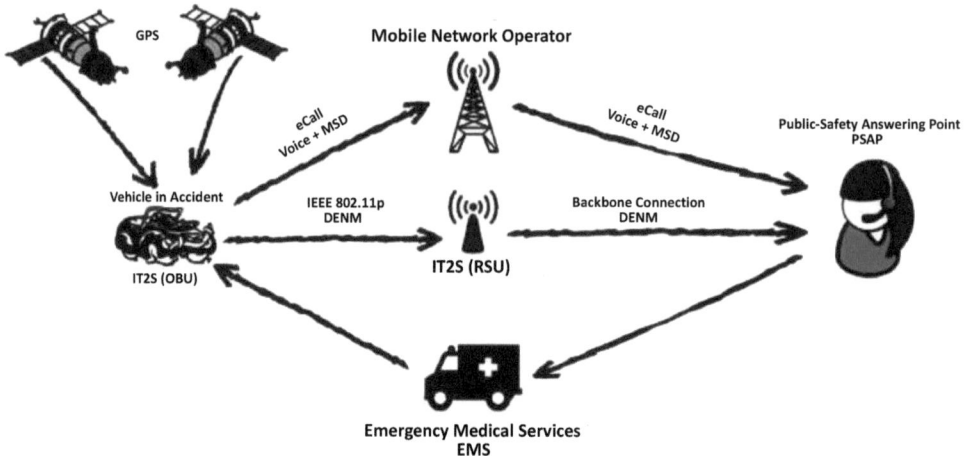

Fig. (2). System architecture.

Javid *et al.* [4] provided a comprehensive analysis of various automatic accident detection techniques, utilizing tools such as smartphones, technologies like GSM and GPS, vehicular ad-hoc networks, and several more. Although ultrasonic sensors have previously been employed in numerous research articles for accident detection, the authors presented a more efficient method of utilizing these sensors. Javid *et al.* proposed the installation of two ultrasonic sensors within the vehicle, and they also discussed the optimal placement for these sensors to enhance their efficiency. Specifically, one sensor is positioned at the front of the car, while the second is placed at the rear. The primary function of an ultrasonic sensor is to calculate the distance between objects by emitting a sound, measuring the time taken for the reflected sound to return, and using this duration to compute the distance. The front sensor is situated on the roof near the windshield. The distance from this point to the car's front bumper is calculated and set as the first predefined threshold for the system. As for the rear sensor, it is mounted on the roof at the back of the car, with the distance to the rear bumper serving as the second predefined threshold. If an object is outside of these predefined thresholds, the system remains inactive. However, if an impact occurs—whether at the front or rear of the vehicle—and it falls within the range of the predefined thresholds, the system activates. It sends a message, which includes relevant information, to the emergency centers *via* GSM and determines the vehicle's location using the GPS module. While the proposed solution is deemed efficient, it is not without limitations, offering opportunities for further research. A critical point to note is that the ultrasonic sensor selected for this system has a limited range of four meters. Therefore, for a vehicle to be compatible with this module, the thresholds must be within this four-meter range; vehicles with thresholds beyond this limit are deemed unsuitable for the system.

Fizzah Bhati *et al.* [2] delineated a system capable of automatic accident detection, utilizing the Internet of Things (IoT) technology. This project was conceptualized with a smart city environment in mind. The primary aim of this research is to harness the full potential of pre-installed smartphone sensors economically, striving to enhance and optimize the transportation system. In this endeavor, speed is identified as a crucial factor for accurate accident detection. The system harnesses various smartphone sensor outputs, including speed, gravitational force, and pressure, to enhance accident detection accuracy. The rationale behind prioritizing speed stems from observed significant differences in environmental conditions during collisions at varying speeds. The document also notes the existence of pre-established systems utilizing smartphones for accident detection. However, these systems' accuracy levels are debatable due to high false positive rates. To address these challenges, this research introduces an IoT-based solution, operational in two distinct phases.

The first phase focuses on accident detection, while the second phase centers on notifying the emergency response centers. The system is wholly dependent on smartphone sensors for accident detection, employing a variety of sensors such as accelerometers, GPS, pressure sensors, and microphones. To facilitate data retrieval from these sensors, a specialized Android application was developed. This application plays a pivotal role in fetching sensor data and transmitting it for further analysis. In this system, accident detection is not the sole priority; equally crucial is the swift notification of accidents and the prompt dispatch of assistance to the location identified during the first phase. Once an accident is detected, the system captures the location, utilizes the phone's cellular data to transmit this information, and initiates the emergency response procedure, as illustrated in Fig. (**3**).

Maleki *et al.* [10] pursued the same objective: to reduce response times in emergency situations. Maleki and his team developed a system, illustrated in Fig. (**4**), designed to detect accidents and relay the necessary information to emergency centers. The research introduces a local-based system, segmented into two main components and embedded in their respective locations. The system operates in a dual manner, proving efficient in its designated functions; it quickly and effectively detects accidents, subsequently sending detailed information about the incident to emergency centers. This is achieved using an array of sensors and modules, similar to those mentioned in previous discussions. The ultimate goal is to reduce the time it takes for emergency responders to arrive at the scene, aiming to save lives that might have previously been lost due to delayed communication. The proposed system consists of several components, strategically embedded in their optimal locations: i) The determination of the accident's location, which is consistently recorded and saved as a text file. ii) The retrieval of signals from the vehicle's airbags. iii) The transmission of the gathered information to the emergency centers. As mentioned earlier, the system operates in two main parts: PART I: This segment is embedded within the vehicle itself and comprises two units—the positioning unit and the wireless information transfer unit. This section is responsible for detecting the accident *via* the airbag system and transmitting the location information to Part II. PART II: This segment is stationed at the rescue center, tasked with receiving the transmitted information and subsequently mapping the accident's location.

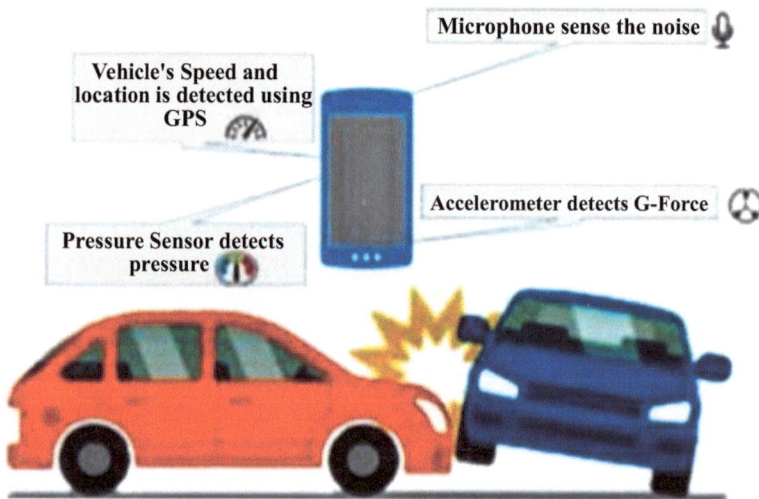

Fig. (3). Components for accident detection.

Khan *et al.* [5] proposed a system for detecting accidents using smartphone sensors. This approach has undergone numerous tests, and the system is showcased with consistent quality. It leverages smartphone sensors to detect accidents and relay information to emergency centers, including tracking the location. However, systems like these often face efficiency challenges due to high false positive rates—they sometimes trigger alerts for incidents that are not critically serious. This research addresses the issue of false positives, proposing a solution that disregards g-force values below 4g. In instances where a false alarm might be triggered, the system provides a 15-second window and an option to cancel the alert if the situation is not critical or no accident has occurred. There is, however, potential for enhancing the system's efficiency by integrating additional sensors, such as gyroscopes, microphones, cameras, *etc.*, alongside the accelerometer.

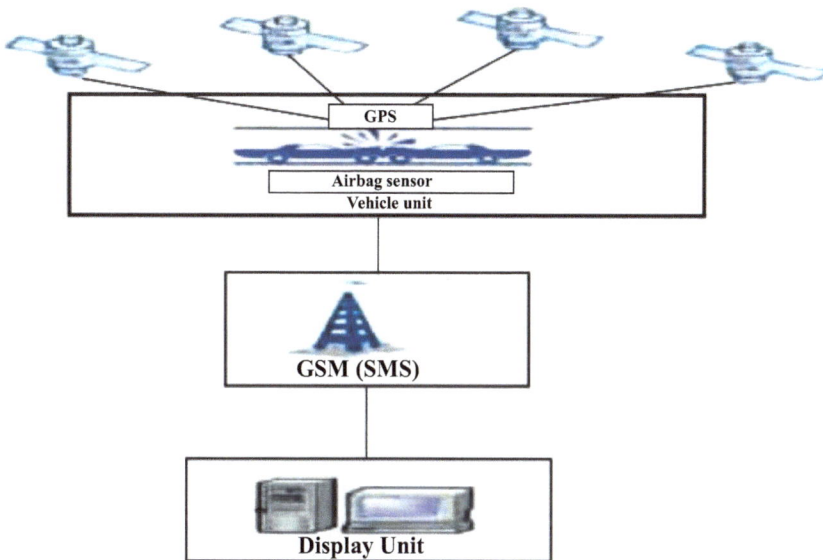

Fig. (4). Accident alarm system.

Part *et al.* [15] introduced a method to assess the speed of a vehicle on the road and its correlation with crash frequency. They developed an algorithm called path analysis to investigate the relationship between speed and collision occurrences, concluding that vehicle speed directly influences the likelihood of a crash. Choi *et al.* [16] presented a deep learning-based ensemble method for crash detection using dashboard camera footage. They collected video and audio data *via* the dashboard camera, employing Gated Recurrent Unit (GRU) and Convolutional Neural Network (CNN) algorithms for accident detection. However, this approach has its drawbacks; the camera's dashboard location makes it susceptible to damage during an accident. Relying solely on the camera, without incorporating any IoT modules, could potentially increase the false positive rate. Pour *et al.* [17] developed an automatic car accident detection method that combines a Convolutional Neural Network (CNN) and Support Vector Machine (SVM). The paper emphasizes the use of a feature selection method, claiming an accuracy rate of 85% during testing. Nevertheless, such a high accuracy rate might not be feasible in real-time scenarios, and the paper provides an extensive discussion of the IoT module.

3. RESEARCH METHODOLOGY

The proposed system is a device that is an automatic accident detection and alerting system, which will determine the accident and automatically tracks the location and can communicate it to the nearest medical centre. The components of the system are shown in Fig. (5). Automatic Accident Detection and Alerting System" comprises three major components, a microcontroller Arduino Uno, a GSM900, and a GPS NEO 6M. The piezoelectric force sensor is also placed inside the system to detect whether an accident is occurring or not. In case of non-severe injury, an SOS button is also placed to inform that the person is alright and doesn't need help.

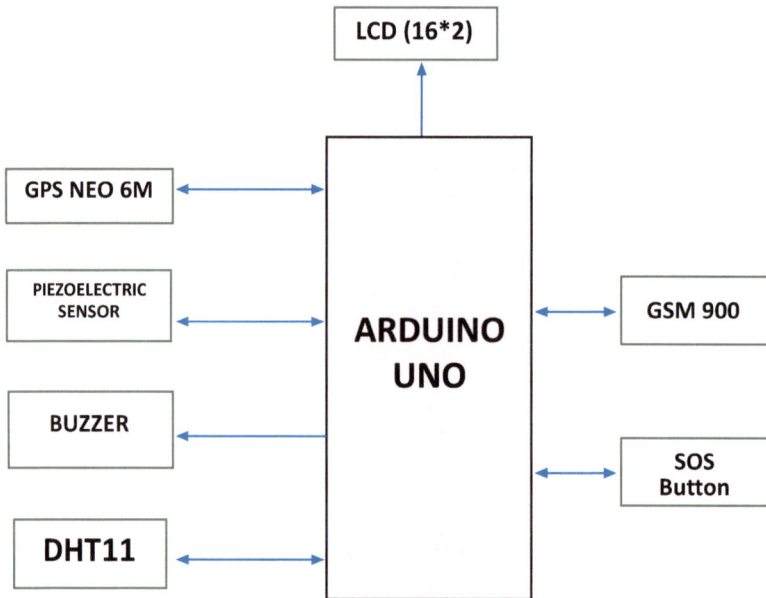

Fig. (5). Overview of the system.

If something hits the sensors that are installed in the vehicle, the system's first part is activated and then the location is captured *via* the GSM module. Then the information regarding the location of the accident and the information regarding the patient's state is sent to a registered phone number through the GSM module. Based on the literature study in this field, it is observed that a few things can be added to this system to make it more efficient and useful, the new features which are not present in the systems discussed earlier by the researcher: - first of all a SOS button so that if the accident is not that severe so the sending of the information can be stopped by pressing the button. On the other end, DHT11 sensors are used to measure the temperature and humidity and AADAAS indicates when the temperature goes increasing by 50 degrees Celsius. It is important to notice that nowadays cars are manufactured with advanced features in order to deal with the power-off situation in new cars during an accident. We are also adding the battery so that all modules work without power and can perform properly.

3.1. Process Flow of the System

On starting the vehicle, first AADAAS (Automatic Accident Detection and Alerting System) will check for its connectivity *i.e.*, the response of sensors, and Internet connectivity, *etc.*, after checking if there is any issue in the connectivity then it will indicate otherwise it will start observing the accident through the sensors embedded in the vehicle all time till the vehicle is in a mobile state. The process flow diagram shown in Fig. (6) shows the flow of data in the AADAAS system. In case, if the vehicle meets an accident, then AADAAS will get into work again. It will turn on the alarm & wait for one minute and will check whether the reset button is pressed or not. If the reset button is pressed within one minute after the vehicle met an accident, then it means the accident is minor and everything is fine and there is no need to help, In this case, AADAAS will again turn off their alarm and will send a message to preregistered no. That person met with an accident but is fine and doesn't require any help and starts observing again for any accident through its sensor.

MOn the other side, if the reset button is not pressed within one minute after the accident, then it means the accident is major, AADAAS will fetch the coordinates of the vehicle through the GPS and GSM and is sent to the emergency or preregistered number. A DHT sensor is also placed in the "AADAAS". DHT is a basic and low-cost sensor for displaying temperature details. After checking the connectivity, it observes the temperature and displays it on the LCD screen. If in a case, the temperature increases by 50 degrees Celsius, then it will be trigger the alarm so that the person can leave the vehicle on time before the vehicle catches fire and can save his/her precious life.

4. RESULTS AND DISCUSSIONS

The prototype of the Automatic Accident Detection and Alerting System equipped with various sensors, *i.e.*, DHT11, piezoelectric force sensor is demonstrated in Fig. (7) having major components such as Arduino Uno, GPS NEO 6M, and GSM900.

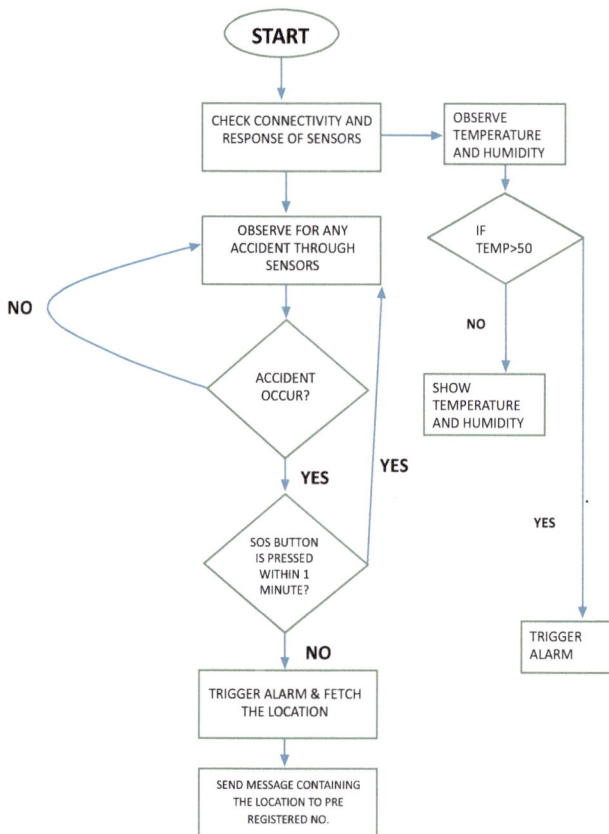

Fig. (6). Process flow of data.

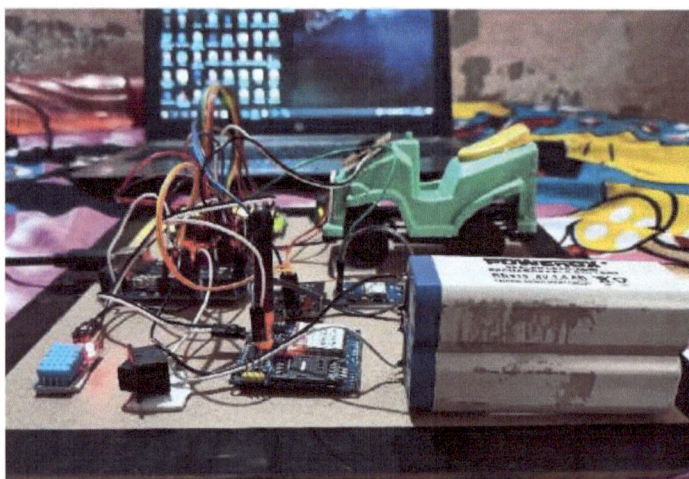

Fig. (7). Model of AADAAS.

Fig. (**8**) depicts the emergency message on LCD, *i.e.*, critical condition and the person needs the help LCD is used to view the details of temperature which is updated at regular intervals in real-time as well as an important message regarding the project as shown in Fig. (**9**).

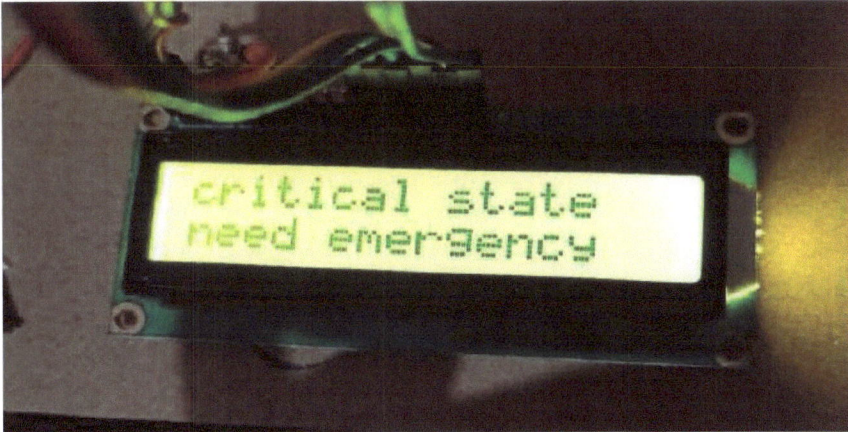

Fig. (8). LCD displays critical state message.

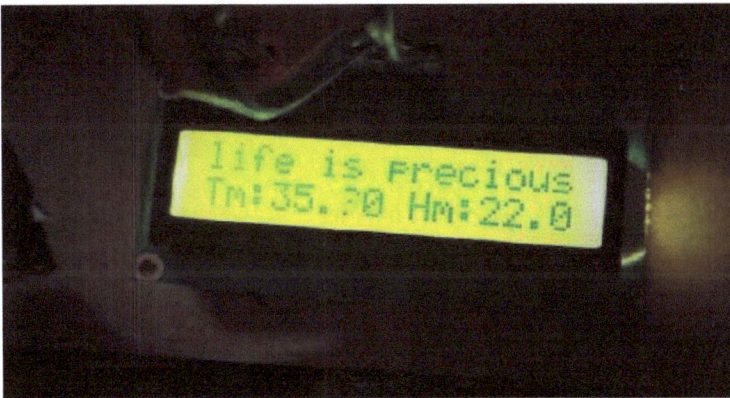

Fig. (9). LCD displays temperature and humidity.

The DHT11 sensor reads the temperature details and checks whether it fails to read from the DHT sensor or not. Also, checks for the piezoelectric force sensor whether this sensor is struck somewhere or not. If it strikes, then the buzzer will start, and the trigger function is called. If the piezoelectric force sensor doesn't strike anywhere, then it displays the temperature details on the LCD with the message that "Life is precious". And it will also turn on the buzzer if the temperature increases. A module is added called when the accident occurs, it displays the message on the LCD that if you are alive press the button and gives us time five seconds. If the button is pressed, then it displays the message on the

LCD that slow drive and accidents occur and sends a message to the phone that the person is in normal condition. If the SOS button is not pressed within five seconds after the vehicle meets an accident, then it shows a message on the LCD, displaying the critical condition, and needs emergency, along with that it will send a message to the registered number having info that the person is in critical condition.

4.1. Demonstration of System

Upon giving power to the system, Arduino Uno boots up. The codes for several components are executed. The calibrated sensors become active, constantly sensing for trigger action. The piezoelectric sensor will be ready to sense the pressure so that it can detect the scenario of the accident and alert accordingly. The GSM module will be all booted up looking for signals and the GPS module will be ready to track the location. As soon as the project gets the power, the LCD will be in a working mode to display the message life is precious and will also be showing the temperature and humidity. As soon as the accident is detected, the GSM module will be ready to send the message.

Now if the accident occurs, the project will be working in two ways. Fig. (**10**) shows that if the accident is detected, the buzzer will start to beep, and the screen will display the message stating "Press the button if you are alive" if, the button is pressed then the system will still send the message to the other unit, but it will be that the person is safe. The messages are shown in Figs. (**11**) and (**12**).

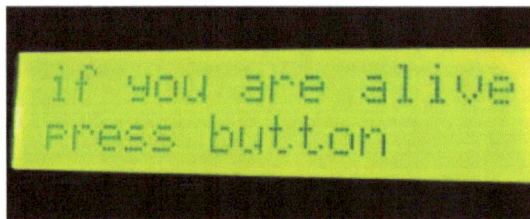

Fig. (10). LCD displaying the message if you are alive, press the button.

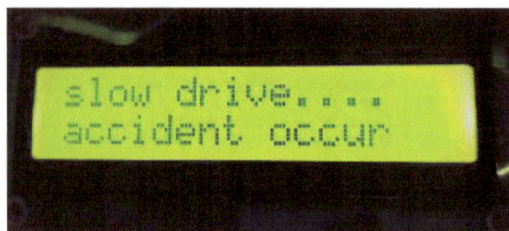

Fig. (11). LCD displaying accidents occurred when the button pressed.

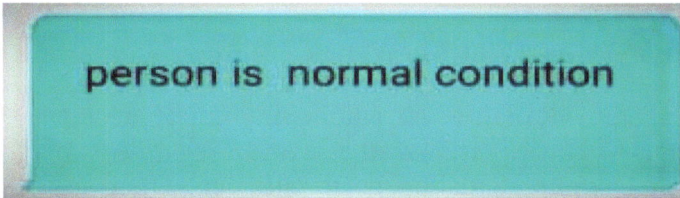

Fig. (12). Screenshot of the message when the button is pressed.

If the accident is too severe and the individual is unable to click the button, then the LCD will display a different message.

Fig. (**13**) depicts the scenario, if the nature of accident is severe and the person involved in the accident is not able to press the button to ensure that he is fine, then this system will send the message to the other desired unit that the person is critical with the location coordinates of the place where the accident occurred.

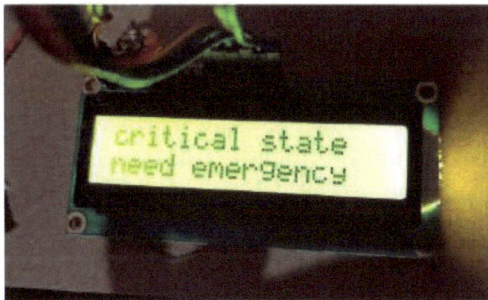

Fig. (13). LCD displaying the critical state when the button is not pressed.

The snapshot of the execution of the system is shown in Fig. (**14**). It shows that the system is working perfectly fine and can detect the accident with all sensors and modules embedded in it and is able to send the message as well with location coordinates so that help can be easily provided to the victim and life can be saved which would be lost if the help will not be available on time.

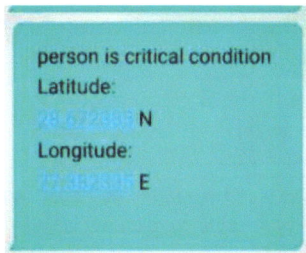

Fig. (14). Screenshot of the message when the button is not pressed.

5. CONCLUSION AND FUTURE WORK

The work presented introduces an automatic vehicle accident detection and alerting system. Countries around the world, regardless of their level of development, are grappling with high death rates due to road accidents. In light of this, scientists and engineers are diligently working to develop systems that can simplify life, automating as many processes as possible. Addressing road accidents requires a system that is sufficiently automatic to tackle the issue effectively. This design enables the detection of accidents swiftly using embedded sensors such as piezoelectric devices, which can also sense environmental conditions like temperature and humidity. The system is capable of sending all necessary information regarding the accident, including the location and a message detailing the situation, to medical centers. Furthermore, this project stands out for being cost-efficient and reliable. With the pressing need for automation across various industries, systems like these are indispensable, making the proposed system highly beneficial to the automotive sector.

The designed system adeptly integrates hardware and software modules, ensuring efficient performance in its primary function: detecting accidents through the designated sensors and sending the location and necessary information *via* GSM and GPS modules. Despite the urgent call for automation and the drive to advance technology beyond its current state, any invention, no matter how groundbreaking, can be improved upon with the introduction of new technologies. With this in mind, the proposed system can be enhanced to operate more efficiently and intelligently. Looking ahead, the incorporation of an expert tracking system could significantly improve the system's precision and utility. This system could track the nearest clinics for minor injuries and hospitals for major accidents. Other potential enhancements to the system include the automatic activation of a fire extinguisher in the event of a fire, achieved through the integrated use of IoT. Furthermore, the adoption of more sophisticated modules could increase the system's precision and simplify the data-gathering process at the accident site. Embedding a camera module into the system could also be considered to enable the sharing of real-time images.

REFERENCES

[1]   A. Francis, S.K. Dharani, P. Manikandan, R.J. Monica, and S.K. Vaishahi, "IoT based accident identification and alerting system", *Int. J. Pure Appl. Math.,* vol. 24, no. 2, pp. 476-502, 2018.

[2]   B. Fizzah, S. Munam Ali, M. Carsten, and A. Saif, "A novel internet of things-enabled accident detection and reporting system for smart city environments", *'Comp.Electr. Eng. Int. J. Islam in Pakistan,* vol. 42, pp. 368-406, 2019.

[3]   B. Fernandes, *Automatic accident detection with multi-modal alert system implementation.* vol. 3. Institute of Telecommunications: Portugal, 2016, pp. 1-11.

[4]   T. Javid, "Automatic road accident detection techniques: A brief survey", *International Journal of Engineering & Technology Graduate School of Engineering Science & Information Technology,* vol. 22, pp. 720-745, 2018.

[5]   A. Khan, F. Bibi, M. Dilshad, and M. Salman, "Accident detection and smart rescue system using android smartphone with real-time location tracking"'", *Int. J. Adv. Comput. Sci. Appl.,* vol. 9, no. 6, pp. 260-272, 2017.

[6]   V. Praveena, A.R. Sankar, S. Jeyabalaji, and V. Srivatsan, "Efficient accident detection and rescue system", *Int.J. Emerg. Trend. Technol. Comp. Sci.,* vol. 3, no. 5, 2014.

[7]   J. James, and S.V. Suryakala, "Advanced vehicle security control and accident alert system", *IACSIT Int. J. Eng. Technol.,* vol. 7, no. 2.8, pp. 404-408, 2018.
[http://dx.doi.org/10.14419/ijet.v7i2.8.10679]

[8]   K.A. Khaliq, S.M. Raza, O. Chughtai, A. Qayyum, and J. Pannek, "Experimental validation of an accident detection and management application in vehicular environment", *Comput. Electr. Eng.,* vol. 71, pp. 137-150, 2018.
[http://dx.doi.org/10.1016/j.compeleceng.2018.07.027]

[9]   Usman Khalil and Tariq Javid, *Automatic Road Accident Detection Techniques: Brief Survey.* vol. 12. Graduate School of Engineering Science & Information Technology: Pakistan, 2017, pp. 366-375.

[10]   J. Maleki, and E. Foroutan, The design of intelligent auto accident alarm system.*Department of Surveying Engineering.* vol. 10. College of Engineering, University of Tehran: Tehran, Iran, 2016, pp. 368-376.

[11]   K.H. Patel, "Utilizing the emergence of android smartphones for public welfare by providing advance accident detection and remedy by 108 ambulances", *Int. J. Eng. Res. Technol.,* vol. 2, no. 9, pp. 1340-1342, 2013.

[12]   S. Zainab, "Car accident detection and notification system using smartphone", *Int. J. Comp. Sci. Mob. Comp.,* pp. 620-635, 2015.

[13]   J. Zaldivar, C.T. Calafate, J.C. Cano, and P. Manzoni, "Providing accident detection in vehicular networks through OBD-II devices and Android-based smartphones", *IEEE 36th Conference on Local Computer Networks,* pp. 813-819, 2011.
[http://dx.doi.org/10.1109/LCN.2011.6115556]

[14]   B. Fernandes, V. Gomes, J. Ferreira, and A. Oliveira, Mobile application for automatic accident detection and multimodal alert.*Vehicular Technology Conference.* IEEE, 2015, pp. 1-5.
[http://dx.doi.org/10.1109/VTCSpring.2015.7145935]

[15]   J.G. Choi, C.W. Kong, G. Kim, and S. Lim, "Car crash detection using ensemble deep learning and multimodal data from dashboard cameras", *Expert Syst. Appl.,* vol. 183, p. 115400, 2021.
[http://dx.doi.org/10.1016/j.eswa.2021.115400]

[16]   H.H. Pour, F. Li, L. Wegmeth, C. Trense, R. Doniec, M. Grzegorzek, and R. Wismüller, *A Machine Learning Framework for Automated Accident Detection Based on Multimodal Sensors.* Cars. Sens, 2022, pp. 1-21.

[17]   E.S. Park, K. Fitzpatrick, S. Das, and R. Avelar, "Exploration of the relationship among roadway characteristics, operating speed, and crashes for city streets using path analysis", *Accid. Anal. Prev.,* vol. 150, p. 105896, 2021.
[http://dx.doi.org/10.1016/j.aap.2020.105896] [PMID: 33285446]

CHAPTER 4

Optimal Election Unequal Clustering Routing Protocol with Improved Tradeoff Function for Wireless Sensor Networks

Ankur[1,*] and Ajay K. Sharma[1]

[1] *Department of Computer Science and Engineering, National Institute of Technology Jalandhar, Jalandhar, Punjab, India*

Abstract: In today's technological landscape, IoT-enabled Wireless Sensor Networks (WSNs) offer significant advantages over traditional networks, particularly when it is used under critical applications. However, network devices are typically limited in terms of their energy source; energy optimization has become a major concern in recent years. As a result, energy-efficient protocols are increasingly being prioritized to extend the network's functionality for a long period. In this chapter, we introduce a clustering routing protocol that operates on an unequal clustering basis. The protocol selects the best route for transmitting data to the sink based on various factors, such as the average residual energy of path sensor nodes, the average distance between nodes, the maximal distance nodes in the current path, and the number of hops. Our simulation results show that the proposed Optimal Energy Unequal Clustering Routing (OEUCR) protocol provides a significant improvement over the existing Energy Efficient Routing Protocol (EERP). Furthermore, we propose an optimal election clustering protocol that provides a new trade-off function based on near density factor and elect metric. Our simulation outcomes demonstrate that this protocol increases the network's functional duration by 6 rounds, reduces energy consumption by 0.727 J per round, and allows the base station to receive 975 more messages. Specifically, the packets received by the base station (BS) increased by 23%, while energy consumption decreased by 21% when using OEUCR instead of EERP.

Keywords: Base station, Cluster, Elect metric, LEACH, Near density factor, TEEN, Wireless sensor networks.

1. INTRODUCTION

Wireless Sensor Networks (WSNs) are used in many applications that require continuous monitoring of a specific region for as long as possible. Since deployed networks have sensors with limited and non-rechargeable energy resources, effec-

---

* **Corresponding author Ankur:** Department of Computer Science and Engineering, National Institute of Technology Jalandhar, Jalandhar, Punjab, India; E-mail: ankurbohora@gmail.com

Samayveer Singh , Manju, Aruna Malik, and Pradeep Kumar Singh (Eds.)

tive and optimized usage of allotted energy is critical. In IoT-enabled WSNs, multiple types of devices receive information and send it to the respective head of the cluster, which sends the data further to the sink with the help of cluster nodes.

To prolong the network's functional duration, clustering is an effective approach that addresses the scalability and lifetime of WSNs. Sensors are divided into various types of clusters based on certain parameters, and only a single node is elected as the cluster head (CH) of the cluster, while the rest of the nodes in the proximity of the cluster heads are called cluster members (CMs). The CM node gathers data from its proximity and directs it to the CH, which aggregates the collected data and forwards it to the base station or sink node [1].

The main aspect of clustering is to extend the total functional duration of the deployed network. Most clustering protocols consider the remaining battery during the process of CHs' selection. However, the authors propose a novel and optimally distributed clustering scheme called the Optimal Election Clustering Protocol (OECP), which introduces a new elect metric during the CH selection phase.

Additionally, the authors introduce the Optimal Election Unequal Clustering Routing Protocol (OEUCRP), which is designed for serial data aggregation applications. It arranges the sensor network by multi-hop routing and unequal clustering.

The manuscript is structured as follows: Section 2 discusses existing research works, while section 3 describes the applied system model. Section 4 provides a detailed description of the proposed clustering protocol, OECP. Section 5 presents the experimental outcomes for OECP when compared with other existing works. Finally, section 6 concludes the manuscript and provides future directions.

2. RELATED WORKS

The authors [2] introduced the LEACH protocol, the first cluster-based routing protocol that allows a fraction p of sensor nodes to serve as CHs, with this role changing over rounds based on the pre-defined area covered by the network. The work discussed an energy efficient hierarchical clustering algorithm for wireless sensor networks that extends the network lifetime [3]. Work [4] proposed the HEED protocol, which identifies CHs with higher remaining energy and lower intra-cluster communication cost. The work discussed an adaptive llc-based and hierarchical power-aware routing algorithm that improves the network lifetime [5]. Authors [6] presented a cluster election and routing protocol based on voting that considers prime factors.

The manuscript [7] proposed EECS, a novel protocol for cluster-based routing that selects CHs based on residual energy and other parameters. Authors [8] introduced the EAP protocol, which selects CHs based on the ratio of residual energy to the average residual energy of all neighbors. In thses studies [9, 10], cost metrics, as well as energy efficiency, are considered. The research work [11, 12] presented a protocol for heterogeneous networks based on a weighted probability approach and a threshold function. The method [13] uses a genetic algorithm-based clustering approach for CH election, mainly designed for movable sinks, and a study [14] proposes a protocol for disaster management systems that use adjustable sensing range and deployment strategies for placing higher energy nodes near the sink to address hotspot problems.

The approach [15] uses a metaheuristic for finding cluster heads efficiently with the help of multiple mobile sinks. Singh *et al.* [16] proposed a nature-inspired clustering algorithm that uses a data aggregation method to reduce energy consumption. The OSEP protocol [17] is an extended version of SEP that incorporates 3-level heterogeneity and modifies energy and threshold formulas. DACHE [18] is an optimized cluster head election routing protocol that extends DEEC by incorporating 3-level heterogeneity and modifying the energy and threshold formula. The sustainable methodology for clustering [19] is an extension of the SEP protocol with a new threshold formula with multiple parameters. The approach [20] maintains sustainability while clustering for data aggregation. Finally, Singh *et al.* discussed hetDEEC, a heterogeneous DEEC protocol that prolongs lifetime in wireless sensor networks by incorporating 3-level heterogeneity and modifying energy and threshold formulas [21, 22]. However, this method also does not provide the lifetime latest defined level.

3. SYSTEM MODEL

A. Network Model:

In this chapter, we consider a sensor network deployed in a square field denoted as A, which possesses the following characteristics:

- The network is assumed to be static and densely deployed, with nodes randomly scattered throughout the field.
- A single sink node, referred to as the base station, is present, and it is located outside of field A.
- Each node is capable of sending data to the base station.
- Nodes are able to compute distances using the received signal strength.
- All nodes are homogeneous and have a fixed communication radius, rc, of 25 meters, similar to Berkeley Motes [12].

All the links are symmetric in nature.

B. Energy Model:

The energy expended to transmit an l-bit message over a distance d is shown below: Thus, to transmit an L-bit message a distance, the radio expands;

$$E_{TX}(l,d) = \begin{cases} lE_{Elec} + lE_{fs}d^2, & if\ d < d_o \\ lE_{Elec} + lE_{amp}d^4, & if\ d \geq d_o \end{cases} \tag{1}$$

And to receive this message, the radio expands:

$$E_{RX}(l) = lE_{Elec} \tag{2}$$

Here, EElec depends on various factors and similarly Efsd2 and Eampd4 too. The value of threshold distance do is given by:

$$d_o = \sqrt{\frac{E_{fs}}{E_{amp}}} \tag{3}$$

4. OPTIMAL ELECTION CLUSTERING PROTOCOL

This chapter proposes a new clustering protocol, called the Optimal Election Clustering Protocol (OECP), that aims to prolong the functional duration of a sensor network by reducing energy consumption during the formation of cluster heads (CHs) from the existing nodes. OECP achieves this by introducing new election metric parameters and a metric-mapping function. The protocol uses a new metric that considers the remaining energy of the node, its distance from the sink, and whether it was within the range of maximum CHs in the previous round.

Unlike some existing clustering protocols such as LEACH, OECP requires CHs to send data directly to the base station but allows for any routing protocol for inter-cluster communication. The protocol operates in rounds, with each round comprising three phases: a setup phase for network initialization, a cluster formation phase, and a data transmission phase [2].

4.1. Setup Phase

During the setup phase, each node broadcasts a HELLO message to its one-hop adjacent nodes to discover neighboring nodes. The HELLO message contains information such as CH messages received in the previous round, the node's ID, remaining battery power, and the calculated overall distance to the base station (BS). Upon receiving a HELLO message, nodes update their one-hop neighbors with this information.

Once this table is completed, node i computes its distance from the base station, dist(i,BS), using the received signal strength. It then calculates the distance factor fid:

$$f_i^d = \frac{dist(i,BS)}{d} \tag{4}$$

$$d = d_1 - d_2 \tag{5}$$

where d_1 is the distance of the farthest node from the sink and d_2 is the distance of the nearest node from the sink. By using this factor node i calculate the distance travel packet to the base station.

Then node i compute the cluster distance (cdii). The distance of cluster c_i is defined as:

$$cd_i = \sum_{j \in n_i} dist(i,j) \tag{6}$$

Then calculate the near-density factor (find):

$$f_i^{nd} = \frac{cd_i}{count(n_i)} \tag{7}$$

By using this factor, node i can be a CH only if it has maximum nodes near it.

Node i stores the last time the message(Mi) is received from CH. Then it computes the CH factor:

$$f_i^{ch} = \frac{N_r - M_i}{N_r} \tag{8}$$

where, N_r is defined as $N_r = \frac{Total\ deployment\ area}{r_c^2} \times no.\ of\ nodes$

This factor helps to find the best CH such that this CH exists in the range of maximum CHs in the previous round. Fig. (1) illustrates the region of current CHs marked in red. Node marked 4 is a node that gets the maximum messages to join the cluster in the previous round, *i.e.*, 4 messages. So, in the current round, this node has the maximum priority of becoming the CH than the nodes marked 3 and 2, which get messages from 3 and 2 regions, respectively, in the previous round.

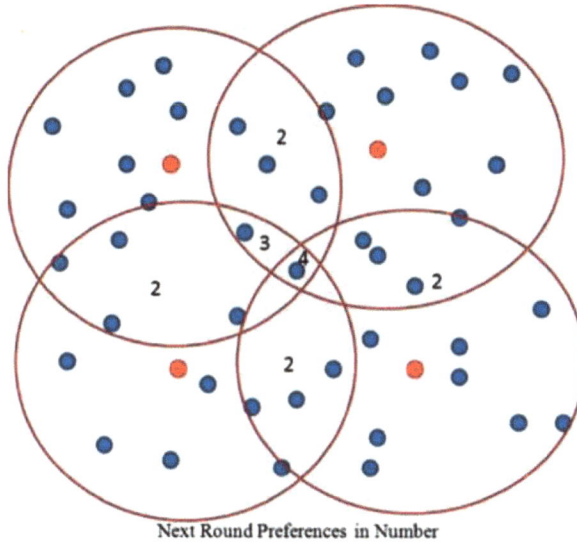

Next Round Preferences in Number

Fig. (1). Representation for CH factor.

By observing (4), (7) and (8), nodeëi formulates the *elect metric*

$$\lambda_i = \frac{E_{avg}}{E_i} \times f_i^d \times f_i^{nd} \times f_i^{ch} \tag{9}$$

where, E_{avg} is the average residual energy of all cluster members.

4.2. CH Election Phase

During this phase, while finding CHs, the highest remaining battery nodes within its proximity are considered to be CH nodes. For node *i*, if $E_i > E_{avg}$, node *i* maps the *elect metric* into an initial time ti using a logarithmic function as in [9]:

$$t_i = \ln\frac{1+x}{1-\lambda_i} \tag{10}$$

Here, x is the random variable that is generated with the help of uniform distribution of intervals [0, 1], Thereafter, ti is unitized and node *i* get its waiting time as in [9]:

$$t_{wt}^i = T_{CH} \times (t_i/c) \tag{11}$$

where T_{CH}: is a fixed system parameter that denotes the maximal time duration for CH selection. c is configured to unitize ti. ti is monotonously increasing when the distance metric is increasing.

After the selection of all CHs, all the remaining sensor nodes decide to join one of the designated CH based on certain rules and policies.

4.3. Data Transmission Phase

In this phase, sensor nodes forward collected information to the designated CHs during the data forwarding task. After receiving the data, CH nodes aggregate this data information and form a single data packet which is further sent to a sink.

5. HETEROGENEOUS OPTIMAL ELECTION UNEQUAL CLUSTERING ROUTING PROTOCOL

In this manuscript, we present a multi-hop hierarchical routing protocol, a CH selects a relay node from its neighbor CHs based on a few factors, which include the number of hops, the node's distance from the BS, and its residual energy. The route selection mechanism is performed by introducing a new route metric for WSNs. Unlike traditional hierarchical routing algorithms, the newly proposed protocol considers the distance of nodes and residual energy as well as the number of hops and density too. The node with the calculated least route metrics is capable of finding routes with a shorter time to compete with other routes. Heterogeneous Optimal election unequal cluster routing protocol called OEUCRP increases the network lifetime for WSN. Simulation results prove that OECURP achieves the desired balance of energy consumption over WSN, and successfully improves the lifetime of the network [21].

5.2. Cluster Setup Phase

The BS broadcasts a control packet that contains the distance of the sink, the distance to the farthest node (d^{max}), and the nearest node (d^{min}) from the sink with associated energy. Every node calculates its d^{bs} (*i.e.*, approximate distance) of the BS based, which directly depends on the received signal strength or by using broadcast packet by the sink. There are three cluster setup phases; neighbor node information collection phase, CH competition phase, and cluster formation phase.

5.2.1. Neighbor Node Information Collection Phase

Each node calculates its local range for managing the cluster size. For i^{th} node, the range is:

$$r_i^l = r_c \times \beta \times d^b \tag{12}$$

Where r_c is the signal range, β is the factor of how many clusters are required in the signal range. In our simulation, the constant factor $\beta = 1/2$, d^b is the broadcast distance that can be calculated as follows:

$$d^b = (1 - \frac{(d^{max} - d^{bs})}{d^{max} - d^{min}}) \tag{13}$$

After that, to find the one-hop neighbors, each node carries out local topology discovery. Each node applies the CSMA\CA protocol to broadcasts a HELLO message in a low range (ril). After receiving a HELLO message from a neighbor sensor node, the node will modify its neighbor table with the received data.

5.2.2. CH Competition Phase

After neighborhood discovery completion, node i calculates the distance factor f^d.

$$f_i^d = \frac{d^{bs}}{d} \tag{14}$$

Where, $d^{bs} = d_{max} - d_{min}$, d_{max} = farthest node distance from the sink, d_{min} = distance of nearest node distance from the sink. By using this factor node i will then calculate the distance for a packet has to travel to reach the BS. Then node i calculates the cluster distance (d_i) as if it's a cluster head and its neighbor nodes are cluster members. Let c_i is a recently formed cluster with the help of cluster head i and all its neighbor nodes (n_i). Thus, one can define the cluster distance cdi as follows:

$$c_{d_i} = \sum_{j \in n_i} dist(i, j) \tag{15}$$

Then calculate the near density factor (fi^{nd})

$$f_i^{nd} = \frac{c_{d_i}}{count(n_i)} \tag{16}$$

By using this factor, node i can be only a CH if it has maximum nodes near it. Node i stores the last received message (Mi) from CH. Then it computes the CH factor:

$$f_i^{ch} = \frac{N_r - M_i}{N_r} \qquad (17)$$

where, $N_r = \frac{Total\ deployment\ area}{r_c^2} \times no.\ of\ nodes$

This factor helps to find the best CH in order to range between many.

By observing (6), (8) and (9), node i get the elect metric:

$$\lambda_i = \frac{E_{avg}}{E_i} \times f_i^d \times f_i^{nd} \times f_i^{ch} \qquad (18)$$

Where E_{avg} is the average residual energy of these nodes which are participating in a particular cluster (*i.e.*, cluster members).

5.2.3. Cluster Formation

Only those nodes that have residual energy greater than that of all its neighbors' average residual energy can participate in the cluster head competition and can be elected as CH. For node *i*, if $E_i > E_{avg}$, node *i* maps the cost metric to an initial time t_i by a logarithmic function

$$t_i = \ln \frac{1+x}{1-\lambda_i} \qquad (19)$$

where x is a random variable with uniform distribution in the interval [0,1], and its function is to minimize the probability of collision that happens when two nodes that are within each other's range gets the same *elect metric*. Thereafter, t_i is unitized and node *i* gets the waiting time as:

$$t_{wt}^i = T_{CH} \times (t_i/c) \qquad (20)$$

Where T_{CH} is a pre-decided system parameter that stands for the maximal time of CH selection. Configuration of *c* is done to unitize t_i. t_i increases when the distance metric increases. The node that has a minor cost metric is going to take less time and has the most probability of being a cluster head. Hence OECURP could balance the energy consumption in the sensor network, which increases the lifetime of the network. During the duration of the backoff time t^i, node i ends the timer when it receives an ADVANCE_CH message and becomes a cluster node and stores the CH node's ID. On the other hand, if the timer expires, node i becomes the CH of the cluster and broadcasts an ADVANCE_CH message to all its neighbors. A non-CH node decides which cluster it has to associate with, after T_{CH} time. Because a non-CH node can receive multiple ADVANCE_CH messages, it tries to join the cluster head that has the highest residual energy by transmitting a JOINING_REQ message. Each cluster head prepares a time-division multiple-access (TDMA) schedule and broadcasts it to all CMs. Once the cluster formation is done, data collection may be started.

5.3. Data Transmission Phase

Intra-cluster Communication: In intra-cluster communication each CM senses and gathers local data from its surroundings and transmits the gathered data to their respective cluster heads. Significantly, all CMs communicate with CHs directly in e cluster.

Inter-cluster Communication: In inter-cluster communication, each CH collects the data from its cluster members and sends the collected data to the BS using multi-hop communication. Here, we introduce an energy-aware multi-hop routing protocol for inter-cluster communication which consists of a route information collection phase and a route formation phase. After each cluster election phase, the sink floods a control packet that is received by all CHs which are in the range of the sink and they in turn again flood the packet forward to the next hop CHs such that the best path is chosen.

Route Information Collection Phase: Each node collects the route information using a flood packet. The flood packet contains the average residual energy of path nodes Eavgr, average distance in between nodes (davgr), max distance node in the current path (dmaxr) and a number of hops (hr). By using this information, CH chooses the best path to sink. CH calculates the route factor for each path as:

Choose the min r^f value path as the next node and send back a control message back to the CH that he is the child of that node.

$$r^f = \left(\frac{E_o - E_{avg}^r}{E_o}\right) \times \left(\frac{d_{avg}^r}{d_{max}^r}\right) \times \left(\frac{h^r}{h_{max}}\right) \qquad (21)$$

After finding the control packet, the last CH updates his routing table.

Route Formation Phase: In this phase, the cluster head collects and aggregates the data from the cluster members, and then transmits this aggregated data *via* multi-hop communication. A cluster head can aggregate the data of its cluster but has to pass data from other CHs if it lies in the route of other CHs to sink.

6. SIMULATION RESULTS

This section of the manuscript demonstrates the analytical results and comparisons of the proposed OECP performed with EADGP by considering the load distribution and network lifetime matrices. We consider sensors (100 in number) over an area of 100m x 100m. We assigned 0.1 J energy to each sensor. Further, the broadcast message (of 200 bits) and data message (of 4000 bits) are assigned. We follow the LEACH model for radio model adoption, and the cluster radius (rc) is initially set to 25 m. A node is said to be dead when it depletes 99.9 percent of energy with respect to the initial energy assigned [4]. In each experiment, every value is an average of 100 values.

As shown in Fig. (**1**), the network functional duration is higher for OECP when compared with EADGP. It happens so because OECP uses the improved cost metric while selecting the CHs in each round. While selecting the CHs during the functionality of OECP, nodes will be preferred with lower cluster cost and higher remaining energy.

Further, the simulation extended, and Fig. (**2**) indicates that the final set or nodes which are alive in OECP are more than those in EADGP. This is because the nearest node to the last CHs moves to the farthest node of the current CH (Fig. **2**). We can see that in the proposed OECP scheme, the first node dies in round 92, while in EADGP, it dies in round 75. In our protocol, 50% of nodes die till round 132, while in the case of EADGP, 50% of nodes die till round 115. In OECP whole network is dead by round 165, and for EADGP, the same happens at round 159. Initially, the difference is more, indicating that the number of alive nodes at the start is more as compared to previous protocols. Fig. (**2**) shows that the frequency of node dying is very low till 50% of the nodes in the network are dead, but after those nodes die more frequently.

In order to observe load balancing among the nodes, we are checking the energy after 75 rounds. Fig. (**3**) shows that the difference between higher energy nodes and lower energy nodes in OECP is less than in EADGP. It shows that the load distribution in the proposed OECP is better than the EADGP.

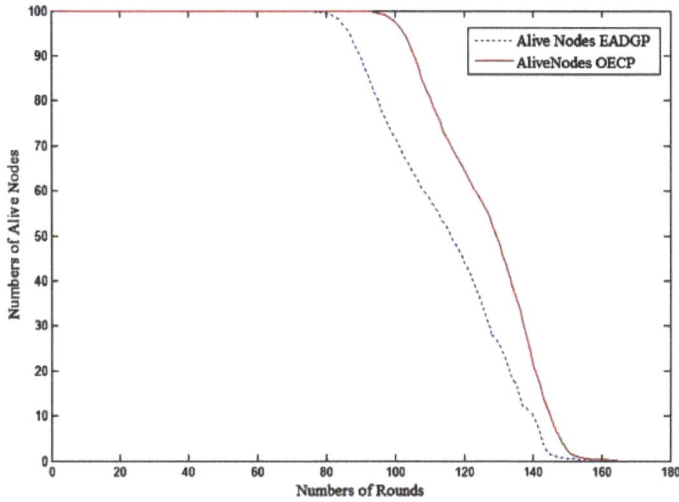

Fig. (2). Network lifetime against the number of rounds for OECP and EADGP.

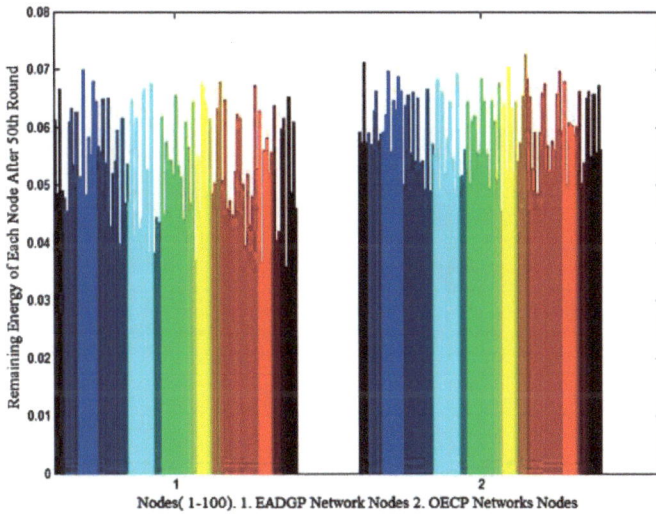

Fig. (3). Each node's remaining energy after fifty rounds for OECP and EADGP.

Fig. (**4**) shows the total residual energy (in Joule) of the whole network after each round. Results show that the energy consumption in EADGP is higher compared to that of OECP. Table **1** depicts the remaining energy for the deployed network after 50, 100 and 150 rounds for OECP and EADGP.

We have analyzed the performance of the OEUCRP and then compared it with EADGP on the basis of load distribution and network lifetime. Assume that over an area of 100m * 100m, 100 wireless sensor nodes are uniformly scattered and the coordinate of BS is (50,175). Each data message is of size 4000 bits, and each broadcast message is of size 200 bits. Each node is allocated .1J energy initially. The parameters of the radio model are the same as in LEACH. The radius of a cluster r_c in a sensor network is 25m. The time from the start of the WSN to the time of the death of the first node in WSN is defined as network lifetime and it is measured in "round". If a sensor node has lost 99.9% of its initial energy then we consider the node as "dead" [5]. We use a random topology of nodes each time we execute the protocol and we execute the protocols 100 times in each experiment.

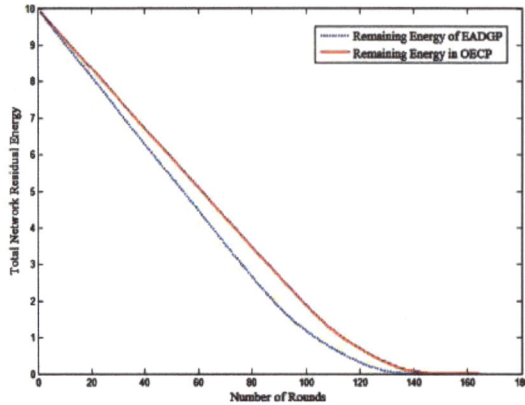

Fig. (4). Network remaining energy (Joule) *vs* number of rounds for OECP and EADGP.

Table 1. Comparison of total residual energy in joule for OECP.

Number of rounds	EADGP	OECP
50	5.6258	6.3416
100	1.2533	1.9861
150	0.0076	0.0548

Fig. (**5**) shows that OEUCRP increases the network lifetime. In the case of EERP, the first node dies at the 77th round, while in the case of OEUCRP, it dies at the 86th round. Similarly, 50% of nodes are dead in EERP and OEUCRP in the 93rd and 114th rounds, respectively. The whole network is dead till round 131 in EERP and till 208 in OEUCRP. In order to observe load balancing among the nodes, we show the remaining energy of nodes after 50 rounds. Fig. (**6**) shows the fluctuations in energy of each node after 50 rounds. If we observe the energy levels, then it is revealed that most of the time, energy is consumed by the higher energy node. It proves that maximum energy consumption is from the higher energy node, and thus, node balancing is done by the new routing scheme in the case of a heterogeneous network. It shows that CH chose the best path among many routes present till BS. Fig. (**7**) shows the total residual energy (in Joule) of the whole network after each round. The result shows that the remaining energy in

EERP is less than the OEUCRP. Table **2** shows the comparison in the remaining energy of the network after 50, 100 and 150 rounds, respectively. The average energy dispersion in EERP is 0.0763 J/Round while 0.0481 J/Round in OEUCRP. That shows in the case of OEUCRP, less energy is consumed per round. The average energy dispersion energy EERP is 36.81% higher than OEUCRP.

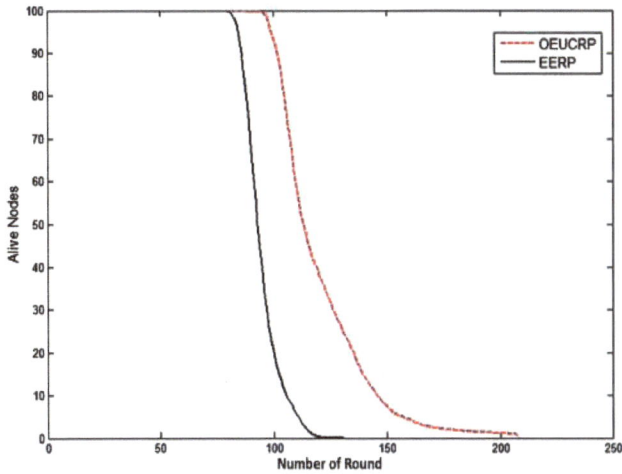

Fig. (5). Network lifetime *Vs* number of rounds for EERP and OEUCRP.

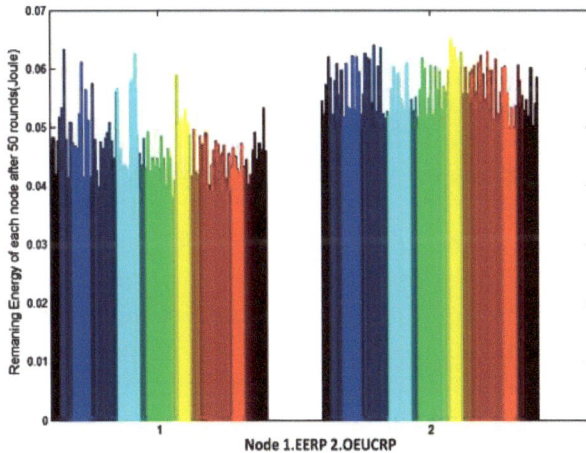

Fig. (6). Each nodes remaining energy after fifty rounds for EERP and OEUCRP.

Table 2. Comparison of total residual energy in joule OECP and EADGP.

Number of round	EERP	OEUCRP
50	4.6062	5.6703
100	0.0866	1.3906
150	0.0000	0.0756

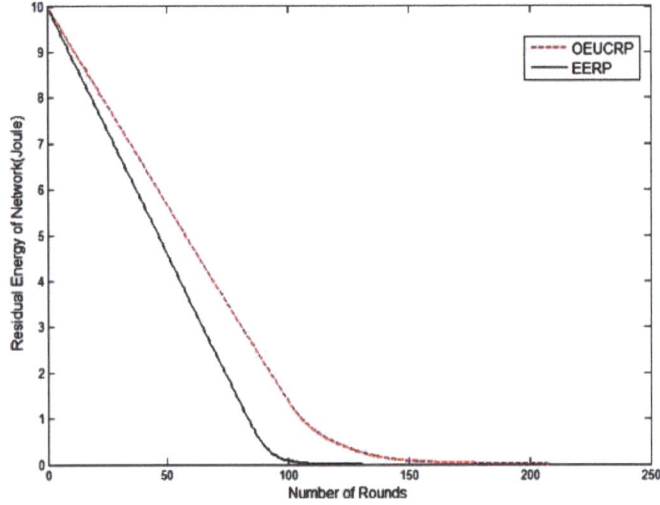

Fig. (7). Network remaining energy (Joule) *vs* a number of rounds for OECP and EADGP.

CONCLUSION

In this chapter, we present simulation results of our proposed Optimal Election Clustering Protocol (OECP) for IoT-enabled Wireless Sensor Networks (WSNs) by modifying the cost metric of the existing EADGP protocol. A comparative study of OECP with EADGP is conducted in a simulation environment using MATLAB. The results reveal that OECP outperforms EADGP, with a 3.77% increase in network lifetime, 9.702% reduction in energy consumption, and 8.25% more messages received at the base station. Our proposed work can be extended to consider the mobility of sinks and sensor nodes. Furthermore, we also present the simulation results of our proposed OEUCRP, which selects the best route based on a trade-off function between distance and hop in the route. Our simulation results show that the network lifetime increases by 76 rounds in the case of OEUCRP, with approximately 23% more packets received at the base station and a 21% reduction in energy consumption. We also observe that the first 50% and 100% of nodes die later in OEUCRP compared to EERP.

REFERENCES

[1]   I.F. Akyildiz, Weilian Su, Y. Sankarasubramaniam, and E. Cayirci, "A survey on sensor networks", *IEEE Commun. Mag.,* vol. 40, no. 8, pp. 102-114, 2002.
        [http://dx.doi.org/10.1109/MCOM.2002.1024422]

[2]   W.B. Heinzelman, A.P. Chandrakasan, and H. Balakrishnan, "An application-specific protocol architecture for wireless microsensor networks", *IEEE Trans. Wirel. Commun.,* vol. 1, no. 4, pp. 660-670, 2002.
        [http://dx.doi.org/10.1109/TWC.2002.804190]

[3]   S. Bandyopadhyay, and E.J. Coyle, "An energy efficient hierarchical clustering algorithm for wireless

sensor networks", *Proceedings of the 22nd Annual Joint Conference of the IEEE Computer and Communications Societies (INFOCOM 2007)*, pp. 1713-1723, 2003.
[http://dx.doi.org/10.1109/INFCOM.2003.1209194]

[4] O. Younis, and S. Fahmy, "HEED: A hybrid, energy-efficient, distributed clustering approach for ad hoc sensor networks", *IEEE Trans. Mobile Comput.*, vol. 3, no. 4, pp. 366-379, 2004.
[http://dx.doi.org/10.1109/TMC.2004.41]

[5] C. Alippi, R. Camplani, and M. Roveri, "An adaptive llc-based and hierarchical power-aware routing algorithm", *IEEE Trans. Instrum. Meas.*, vol. 58, no. 9, pp. 3347-3357, 2009.
[http://dx.doi.org/10.1109/TIM.2009.2016781]

[6] R. Zimmermann, "An energy-efficient voting-based clustering algorithm for sensor networks", *In Proceedings of the Sixth International Conference on Software Engineering, Artificial Intelligence,Networking and Parallell Distributed Computing and First ACIS International Workshop on Self-Assembling Wireless Networks (SNPD/SA WN 2005), pp. 444-451*, 2005.

[7] M. Ye, C. Li, G. Chen, and J. Wu, "An energy efficient clustering scheme in wireless sensor networks", *Ad Hoc Sens. Wirel. Netw.*, vol. 3, pp. 99-119, 2007.

[8] M. Liu, Y. Zheng, J. Cao, G. Chen, L. Chen, and H. Gong, "An energy-aware protocol for data gathering applications in wireless sensor networks", *Proceedings of IEEE International Conference on Communications (ICC 2007)*, pp. 3629-3635, 2007.
[http://dx.doi.org/10.1109/ICC.2007.598]

[9] Z.G. Sun, Z.W. Zheng, S.J. Xu, and S.H. Chen, "Energy-aware data gathering protocol for wireless sensor networks", *In Computer Science and Information Technology (ICCSIT), 3rd IEEE International Conference*, vol. 7, pp. 103-107, 2010.

[10] S. Olariu, and Q. Xu, "Information assurance in wireless sensor networks", *In IEEE Proceedings Parallel and Distributed Processing Symposium, 19th IEEE International*, 2005.
[http://dx.doi.org/10.1109/IPDPS.2005.257]

[11] A.A. Abbasi, and M. Younis, "A survey on clustering algorithms for wireless sensor networks", *Comput. Commun.*, vol. 30, no. 14-15, pp. 2826-2841, 2007.
[http://dx.doi.org/10.1016/j.comcom.2007.05.024]

[12] S. Singh, and A. Malik, "Heterogeneous energy efficient protocol for enhancing the lifetime in WSNs", *Int. J. Inform. Technol. Comp. Sci.*, vol. 8, no. 9, pp. 62-72, 2016.
[http://dx.doi.org/10.5815/ijitcs.2016.09.08]

[13] A.S. Nandan, S. Singh, and L.K. Awasthi, "An efficient cluster head election based on optimized genetic algorithm for movable sinks in IoT enabled HWSNs", *Appl. Soft Comput.*, vol. 107, p. 107318, 2021.
[http://dx.doi.org/10.1016/j.asoc.2021.107318]

[14] S. Singh, A.S. Nandan, A. Malik, N. Kumar, and A. Barnawi, "An energy-efficient modified metaheuristic inspired algorithm for disaster management system using WSNs", *IEEE Sens. J.*, vol. 21, no. 13, pp. 15398-15408, 2021.
[http://dx.doi.org/10.1109/JSEN.2021.3074497]

[15] P. Gupta, S. Tripathi, and S. Singh, "Energy efficient hotspot problem mitigation techniques using multiple mobile sink in heterogeneous wireless sensor network", *Int. J. Commun. Syst.*, vol. 33, no. 18, p. e4641, 2020.
[http://dx.doi.org/10.1002/dac.4641]

[16] S. Singh, "An energy aware clustering and data gathering technique based on nature inspired optimization in WSNs", *Peer-to-Peer Netw. Appl.*, vol. 13, no. 5, pp. 1357-1374, 2020.
[http://dx.doi.org/10.1007/s12083-020-00890-w]

[17] S. Singh, P.K. Singh, and A. Malik, "OSEP: An optimized stable election protocol in heterogeneous wireless sensor networks", *The International Conference on Recent Innovations in Computing*, pp.

235-251, 2020.

[18]   A. Malik, S. Singh, and P.K. Singh, "DACHE: A data aggregation-based effective and optimized cluster head election routing protocol for HWSNs", *The International Conference on Recent Innovations in Computing,* pp. 275-292, 2020.

[19]   S. Singh, *A Clustering-Based Optimized Stable Election Protocol in Wireless Sensor Networks.* Applications in Ubiquitous Computing, 2020, pp. 157-176.

[20]   S. Singh, "A sustainable data gathering technique based on nature inspired optimization in WSNs", *Sustainable Computing: Informatics and Systems,* vol. 24, p. 100354, 2019.
[http://dx.doi.org/10.1016/j.suscom.2019.100354]

[21]   S. Singh, and A. Malik, "hetDEEC: Heterogeneous DEEC protocol for prolonging lifetime in wireless sensor networks", *J. Inform. Optimiz. Sci.,* vol. 38, no. 5, pp. 699-720, 2017.
[http://dx.doi.org/10.1080/02522667.2016.1220083]

[22]   S. Chand, S. Singh, and B. Kumar, "Heterogeneous HEED protocol for wireless sensor networks", *Wirel. Pers. Commun.,* vol. 77, no. 3, pp. 2117-2139, 2014.
[http://dx.doi.org/10.1007/s11277-014-1629-y]

CHAPTER 5

Analysis and Performance Evaluation of Routing Protocols using Sink Mobility in IoT-enabled Wireless Sensor Networks

Samayveer Singh[1,*] and **Aruna Malik**[1]

[1] *Department of Computer Science and Engineering, Dr. B. R. Ambedkar National Institute of Technology, Jalandhar, Punjab, India*

Abstract: The effect of sink mobility on the improved dual-hop routing protocol (IDHR) and multiple data sink-based energy-efficient cluster-based routing protocol (MEEC) is taken into consideration. Sink mobility can be introduced into the network to prevent the creation of hotspots. The data sinks receive data from cluster heads which further collect data from the member nodes of the respective clusters. The cluster head (CH) performs data aggregation and sends the orchestrated data to the sink. The CH selection in IDHR and MEEC is done by taking into account the node density parameter along with other parameters, such as energy and distance between the node and the sink. In MEEC, multiple data sinks are used to resolve the burden on the relaying nodes involved in data transmission as well as to curb the hotspot problem. The movement of sinks is controlled and managed through the proposed approach, *i.e.*, Sink Mobility based on CH Energy (SMCHE). The node density factor proves to be good for the energy preservation of nodes as it takes into account the average communication distance between the nodes and respective CH. The simulation results show that the network lifetime of the proposed approach is increased by 268%, 191%, 27%, and 17% when compared to MEEC, IDHR, DRESEP and TSEP, respectively.

Keywords: Routing protocols, Cluster heads, Energy efficiency, Network lifetime, Mobile sinks.

1. INTRODUCTION

The wireless sensor nodes are tiny, battery-operated devices since it is not feasible to maintain the main power supply to their deployment site. So, power to these wireless sensor nodes is generally provided through primary batteries.

---

[*] **Corresponding author Samayveer Singh:** Department of Computer Science and Engineering, Dr. B. R. Ambedkar National Institute of Technology, Jalandhar, Punjab, India; E-mail: samayveersingh@gmail.com

Samayveer Singh , Manju, Aruna Malik, and Pradeep Kumar Singh (Eds.)

These sensor nodes have processing and communicating functionalities that enhance their network-creating function in any attended or unattended (hostile/ remote) areas. A sensor node consists of three main components:

- The sensing section comprises the sensor itself, which is based on a particular technology. The variety of technologies means you can select a sensor technology that is most suited to the application required.
- The processing circuitry converts the physical variable into an electrical variable to process.
- The signal output contains the electronics connected to a control system.

The sensor nodes have only a limited energy resource (batteries), therefore, this energy should be dissipated only precisely to acquire a higher network lifetime. The battery consumption of a sensor node is directly dependent on how the nodes communicate with each other or with the sink and is utilized accordingly. The sensor nodes form a wireless network to collect data from their surroundings and then coordinate themselves according to the type of application that is needed to be performed. Later, these nodes send the aggregated data to the data sink or the base station, which helps in achieving the respective task [1]. The network formed as a result of the above is termed a wireless sensor network (WSN).

It is impossible to change or recharge the sensor nodes' batteries when they are used in unsupervised or remote locations. Therefore, it is assumed that when the battery of a node is exhausted, it is assumed to be dead, and if it happens to all other nodes, then the whole network becomes inactive and is considered to be dead. Therefore, the main concern is to enhance the network lifetime and the stability period (number of rounds covered until the first node is dead) of the network. The applications where wireless sensor network has an important role to play are only limited in the human imagination. It helps in monitoring the surroundings and therefore finds applications in remote healthcare, disaster management, environment, and industrial monitoring, reconnaissance and targeting system, battlefield surveillance, air pollution, and agricultural monitoring [2].

Problems in WSNs: The topology of the network decides the placement of the sink inside/outside the network. In some remote applications, where the area under consideration is quite large, the sink is needed to be placed outside that area and eventually, communication takes place through multi-hoping. A moment comes during transmission when the relaying nodes are completely exhausted and out of energy. As a result, the data transmission to the sink breaks, and a hot spot is created. This condition is termed as a hot-spot problem [3, 4]. This is due to the excessive relaying load on the nodes closer to the sink. When the single sink is operating, the nodes perform multi-hop communication and face the following problems:

- Procrastination in data delivery is the result of the congestion formed around the single sink.
- Scalability gets affected due to the large size of the network, which physically ends up increasing the communicating distance between nodes and the sink.
- The single sink of the network is prone to the 'No Communication' condition whenever sink failure occurs due to any particular reason, which makes the network dependent on a single sink.
- Frequent selection or frequent rotation of relay nodes gives rise to the number of overheads leading to network degradation.

It is worth noting that when only single-hop communication from CH to sink is implemented, there is no hot-spot problem. To implement single-hop communication in large area networks, the only possible and appropriate solution that also considers balancing energy is employing multiple data sinks. It is concluded from the above study of the heterogeneous protocols that they have employed a single sink in their approach toward acquiring network longevity. In some applications, where the network area is hostile and placement of sinks is supposed to be done outside the network, the scenario of multiple data sinks becomes significant. Some of the terminologies are given as follows:

- **Sink:** The data sink is a term used to describe a computer or any other medium capable of receiving data.
- **Cluster head:** A node in a cluster that is responsible for collecting data from sensors in its cluster and relaying these data to the sink.
- **Node density:** Node density describes the portion of the potential connections in a certain proximity.
- **Heterogeneous wireless sensor network:** A network of the wireless sensor having nodes of different energy capacity
- **Multi-hop routing:** Multi-hop routing is a type of communication in radio networks in which the network coverage area is larger than the radio range of single nodes. Therefore, to reach some destination, a node can use other nodes as relays.

The rest of the chapter is organized as follows: Section 2 discusses the related work similar to the routing protocols in IoT enabled wireless sensor networks. The system model is discussed in Section 3 and the proposed work is discussed in Section 4. The performance analysis is given in Section 5 and the paper is concluded in Section 6.

2. RELATED WORK

Lots of research work has been reported in order to contribute to the network stability and longevity of HWSN. The cluster-based routing has proved to be crucial in minimizing the number of transmissions of sensor nodes to a sink and therefore enhancing the lifetime. The clustering also provides scalability to the network, which makes it possible to extend the physical boundaries of the network with respect to the significant number of nodes deployed in the wireless network. The literature work reported till now reviews the research contributions made in three different aspects. These aspects are:

- CH selection for HWSN to implement energy-efficient routing.
- Various routing strategies were encountered to curb the hot-spot problem.
- The routing techniques take into account single and multiple data sinks in HWSN.

Some of the research works have implemented the frequent rotation of relay nodes for their dual-hop or multi-hop communication in the network. However, it is noted that the systematic rotation of relay nodes still causes an increase in overheads which further depletes their energy and has negative consequences.

Heinzelman *et al.* [1] proposed a distributed cluster-based routing protocol for WSNs, called low-energy adaptive clustering hierarchy (LEACH). The operation of LEACH is divided into rounds. To balance energy consumption, LEACH randomly chooses a fraction p of all sensor nodes to serve as CHs and rotates this role among the sensor nodes in each round. p is a pre-determined system parameter, and its value depends on the size of the sensor network. Hybrid energy-efficient distributed (HEED) [2] is one of the effective data gathering protocols without the size and density of the sensor network known. HEED selects tentative CHs based on the node's residual energy, and final CHs are elected according to the intra-cluster communication cost. A novel voting-based clustering algorithm (YCA) is proposed in a study [3]; sensor nodes vote for their neighbors to select CHs. A node with high residual energy will get more votes and has more chance to become a CH.

In a study [4], the energy-efficient clustering scheme (EECS) first selects a constant number of candidate nodes and then lets them compare for CHs according to the remaining energy of the candidates. In a paper [5], the authors consider the node clustering problem as a new cost metric is presented during the CH selection phase. The new metric considers not only the residual energy of nodes but also energy efficiency and proposes an energy-aware data gathering protocol (EADGP). Singh *et al.* discuss heterogeneous energy efficient protocol for enhancing the lifetime in WSNs [6]. This method uses a weighted election probability and threshold function for calculating the clusters in three levels of heterogeneity. However, it does consider the data collection from cluster heads to sinks.

Nandan *et al.* discussed an efficient cluster head election based on an optimized genetic algorithm for movable sinks in IoT-enabled HWSNs [7]. This method discusses genetic algorithm-based clustering with a higher energy node deployment strategy. This method also uses stable and movable sinks for analyzing the performance. Singh *et al.* discuss an energy-efficient modified metaheuristic-inspired algorithm for disaster management systems using WSNs [8]. This approach uses the adjustable sensing range along with the stable and movable sensing range. It also uses the deployment strategy for placing the higher energy nodes near the sink which deals with the hotspot problem. Gupta *et al.* discuss energy-efficient hotspot problem mitigation techniques using multiple mobile sinks in heterogeneous wireless sensor networks [9]. This approach uses a metaheuristic to find the cluster heads efficiently with the help of multiple mobile sinks. This method solves the hot spot problem up to some extent.

Singh *et al.* discussed an energy aware clustering and data gathering technique based on nature-inspired optimization in WSNs [10]. The nature-inspired optimization is used for cluster head election. This method also uses the data aggregation method, which reduces energy consumption. However, this shows good results for the effectiveness of the method. Singh *et al.* discussed OSEP: an optimized stable election protocol in HWSNs [11]. This approach is the extension of the SEP by incorporating 3-level of heterogeneity and modifying the energy and threshold formula. However, this method does not provide the lifetime latest defined level. Malik *et al.* discussed DACHE: a data aggregation-based effective and optimized cluster head election routing protocol for HWSNs [12]. This approach is the extension of the DEEC by incorporating 3-level of heterogeneity and modifying the energy and threshold formula. This method also uses the data aggregation method, which reduces energy consumption. However, this method does not provide enough lifetime as required in such types of networks. Singh discusses a clustering-based optimized stable election protocol in WSNs [13]. This method uses a new threshold formula with multiple parameters. It is an extension of the SEP protocol.

Singh *et al.* discussed a sustainable data gathering technique based on nature-inspired optimization in WSNs [14]. The nature-inspired optimization is used for cluster head election and also uses the data aggregation method which reduces energy consumption. This method maintains its sustainability. Singh *et al.* discuss hetDEEC: Heterogeneous DEEC protocol for prolonging lifetime in wireless sensor networks [15]. This approach is the extension of the DEEC by incorporating 3-level of heterogeneity and modifying the energy and threshold formula. However, this method does not provide the lifetime latest defined level. Chand *et al*. discussed heterogeneous HEED protocol for WSNs by adding 3 levels of network heterogeneity [16]. This paper uses the fuzzy logic-based clustering system by considering the parameters namely: distance, residual energy, and density of the nodes in a cluster. However, this method performs well compared to the original HEED protocol.

Improved dual-hop routing (IDHR): The reason for developing IDHR was that it is required in large area deployment applications [17]. Here, the single sink is placed in the middle of the network inside the network. Dual hop communication is established by defining a radius (circular) inside the network that is based on the average distance between sinks and nodes and therefore dual hops are established. Multiple data sink-based energy efficient clustering-based routing (MEEC): MEEC was introduced to handle networks that comprise multiple data sinks [17]. In the setup phase, CH selection is carried out and in the steady phase, the solution to the hot-spot problem is implemented. In MEEC, setup phase is similar to the IDHR protocol which helps in network formation. Sink placement in MEEC differs as compared to that of IDHR due to the introduction of multiple sinks in MEEC. The placement of four data sinks is done systematically in the center of each boundary at 10 m distance outside the square-shaped region of each side from the boundary is done.

3. SYSTEM MODEL

A few network assumptions were adopted in routing protocols that will be operated in HWSN:

- Randomly deployment of nodes in rectangular-shaped region of area A. The nature of the nodes is static, having its identification number.
- There are 3 heterogeneity levels of sensor nodes: normal, intermediate, and advanced. Advanced nodes have the highest energy, normal has the least.
- The location of sensor nodes is not known as they don't have any GPS chips attached to them.
- After the deployment of nodes, the nodes cannot be recharged as there won't be any recharging source available. So, energy preservation is a must for extending the battery lifetime.
- The allocation of data sinks is done after the random deployment of sensor nodes. HELLO message is broadcasted by each sink which in turn is acknowledged by all the nodes. Also, the HELLO_neighbour message is

broadcasted by each node to all the nodes in the communication range. The exchange of these messages helps in computing the distance between each node and also with sinks.

• Fusion of data after receiving from neighbor nodes is done and the generation of one fused packet is done.

• The systematic allocation of 4 sinks is done in MEEC protocol around each boundary. Adequate power supply for the sinks making energy constraints on them. These sinks are similar to one another, enriched with computation, memory, and energy.

• Consumption of energy is done by sensor nodes by following a fundamental radio energy model having a radio link that is symmetric in between them.

• Communication among nodes is wireless and secure. Issues related to security are beyond the scope of the chapter.

4. PROPOSED METHOD

The objective of the chapter is to perform an analysis of the Mobility of Sinks in the two protocols IDHC and MEEC. Working and different phases of protocols have already been explained. The analysis will help us to understand the effect of the mobility of the sink on the network longevity and the behavior of the nodes. This work can be extended to predict the pattern of energy degradation of each node and whole network under the sink movement in single and multiple sinks. An extension can also be made in analyzing the factors that are responsible for choosing the cluster head of the network sector and also to improvise the equation for calculating the direct communication of the node with the sink, thus reducing the network degradation through the Hotspot Problem. This can also be extended to study and determine the best region of mobility for improved network performance and to understand the sink placement strategy in the region where human intervention is difficult.

In this work, the default sink location is (50, 50), whereas a random sink location is also considered and the performance of the network is evaluated by placing the sink at different locations. The results of this have been shown in the report ahead.

In this, mobility is introduced along the x-axis keeping the y-axis at 50 coordinates. The movement type is linear and to and fro movement. The parameters that are used to introduce mobility along the x-axis are given as follows: (1) the upper bound is the maximum position to which the sink can reach before reversing the direction, (2) the lower bound is the minimum position to which the sink can reach before reversing the direction, (3) change refers to the incremental change each round of the algorithm undergoes. The number of steps sink will change its direction can be calculated as follows:

direction = absolute (upper bound - lower bound) / change

The initial sink position can also affect the network performance and the upper bounds, and lower bounds need to be changed accordingly. Similarly, the mobility along the y-axis is as follows: Initial sink location is the x-axis and y-axis (50, 50). Here, mobility is introduced along the y-axis, keeping the x-axis to 50 coordinates. The movement type is linear, up and down movement. The number of steps sink will change its direction can be calculated as follows:

direction = absolute (upper bound - lower bound) / change

The initial sink position can also affect the network performance and the upper bounds and lower bounds need to be changed accordingly.

In the sink mobility process of the proposed work, the process initiates with the knowledge of all active nodes in the network, if any active node is there, then the sink mobilization process starts. Three different cases are considered for the same and that are discussed above. After the sink mobilization cluster heads process starts. At the last update energy process start and calculate the remaining energy for the next round. The expanding sink mobilization process of the proposed work where first of all, current sink coordinates are checked and are increased by the required change. Algorithm 1, Sink Mobility based on CH Energy (SMCHE) outlines these steps executed by the mobile sink.

Algorithm 1. Sink Mobility based on CH Energy (SMCHE).

Input: Number of CHs= n , Area, Mobile Sinks Location $(mSink\_X_i, mSink\_Y_i)$
Output: New position of Mobile Sink

1 **Begin**
2 Set of CHs' energy $[CH\_E_1, CH\_E_2, ..., CH\_E_n]$
3 $Min_{Energy} = CH\_E_1$
4 $CH\_id = 1$;   /* The value of the identifier assigned to the CH with the lowest energy at the outset. */
5 Get the positions of CHs (CH_X_i, CH_Y_i);   /* where $i \in 1$ to n */
6 **for** each CH_i $i \in 2$ to n
7   Get (CH_X_i, CH_Y_i, CH_E_i)
8   **if** $CH\_E_i < Min_{Energy}$
9        $Min_{Energy} \leftarrow CH\_E_i$
10       $CH\_id = i$
11   **end if**
12 **end for**
13 $CH\_id_{Lenergy} = CH\_id$
14 Get current position of mSink $(mSink\_X_i, mSink\_Y_i)$;   /* Initially the coordinates are (0,0) */
15 Update the mSink$(mSink\_X_i, mSink\_Y_i)$
      using $mSink\_X_i = mSink_{X_i} + (CH_{id_{Lenergy}}(CH_{X_i}, CH_{Y_i})/n)$
          $mSink\_Y_i = mSink\_Y_i + (CH_{id_{Lenergy}}(CH_{X_i}, CH_{Y_i})/n)$
16 **Return** mSinks moves towards the new generated $(mSink\_X_i, mSink\_Y_i)$ in step 15
17 **Stop**

Dividing the network into clusters presents a promising solution for network management. Each cluster acts as a subnetwork, with a designated cluster head (CH) responsible for collecting and transmitting sensed data to the sink. The mobile sink first identifies the cluster with the CH possessing the lowest energy compared to other CHs.

Once the CHs and their residual energies have been identified and shared with the sink, the sink compares the residual energies of the CHs to locate the cluster corresponding to the CH with the lowest energy level. If the sink moves closer to the CH with the lowest energy level, it saves its energy and can continue to operate for a longer time. This is because the energy consumed by a node depends greatly on the distances between the node and its receivers. However, if the sink visits a cell containing the CH with the lowest energy, the other CHs must transmit data over long distances, which can result in packet loss. To minimize packet loss, we propose the following step for the mobile sink.

Once the cluster with the CH possessing the lowest energy has been identified, the sink calculates the centroid between the CHs in terms of distance and energy. The sink moves towards the location of the lowest energy CH. This enables the sink to position itself close to the cluster with the lowest energy CH and at an approximately equal distance from the other CHs. The CH with the lowest energy then only needs to send its packets over a short distance, helping it conserve energy and prolong its lifespan. Once the round is complete, the sink shares its position with the CHs and initiates the dissemination of sensed data. Each CH then transmits its aggregated packets to the sink at its respective location.

5. EXPERIMENT SETUP AND RESULTS ANALYSIS

In this study, we have considered three different cases for recording the performance of the algorithm in the mobility scenarios: in case 1: mobility along the x-axis under different speed factors and varying max and min ranges are considered, in case 2: mobility along the y-axis under different speed factors and keeping max= 80 and min = 20 range are considered, whereas in case 3: zero mobility but different sink positions. MATLAB language is used for implementation. It is widely used in the wireless communication domain to reduce development time, simulate the wireless network and analyze its efficiency, eliminate design problems early, and streamline testing and verification. In this chapter, we proposed the mobility of sink in the network of 100 m × 100m along both axes. We implemented the mobility of the sink in the linear direction. We also tested the sink at a random position instead of its default location at the center, *i.e.*, (50, 50). The moving trajectory of the mobile sink is well-scheduled and it owns unlimited energy and communication range. SNs keep on sensing the data continuously but are unable to transmit it until the threshold value is reached. Simulation parameters are given in Table **1**, which are used for the simulation purpose.

Table 1. Simulation parameters.

Parameters	Value
Network Deployment	Random
Communication Approach	TDMA
Threshold Formula	Probability based
Network Area Size, Number of Nodes (N)	100 × 100 m^2, 100
Number of data sinks for IDHR and MEEC	1 and 4
Initial energy of nodes (in Joules) (Eo)	1
Energy heterogeneity Node Type	3-level; normal, intermediate and advanced nodes
Energy fraction of intermediate nodes (β) and advanced nodes (α)	β = 1, α=2
Number of intermediate nodes (m) and advanced nodes fraction (mo)	m = 0.2, m o =0.1
Energy required for running transmitter and receiver E elc	50nJ/bi
Threshold distance (d o)	87m
Sink Placement (IDHR)	(50,50)

Alive Node: The nodes that propagate packets until they exhaust all their energy are called alive nodes. Fig. (**1**) represents the simulation result for alive nodes for multiple sinks with reference to the number of rounds. The simulation results show that the number of alive nodes per round is significantly higher in the proposed approach. This is because, in our approach, nodes consume less energy for packet transfer compared to other methods, due to the energy-aware movable sink. The proposed method is able to transmit the packet for a long time due to the extended lifetime of the network. The network lifetime is increased by 268%, 191%, 27%, and 17% when compared to MEEC, IDHR, DRESEP, and TSEP, respectively.

Number of packets sent to BS: The capacity to transfer collected data in the network lifespan is determined by the number of packets transferred to the BS. As shown in Fig. (**2**), the number of packets sent to the BS increases as the network lifetime is extended. During the initial rounds, packet transmission follows a linear trend. The results of the experiment depicted in Fig. (**2**) that indicates that proposed approach has achieved a higher packet transfer rate compared per round in comparison with MEEC, IDHR, DRESEP and TSEP.

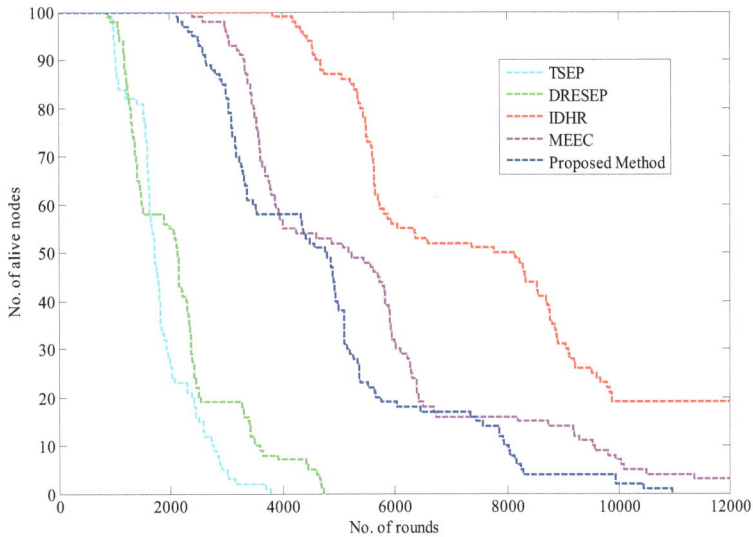

Fig. (1). Number of alive nodes V/s number of rounds.

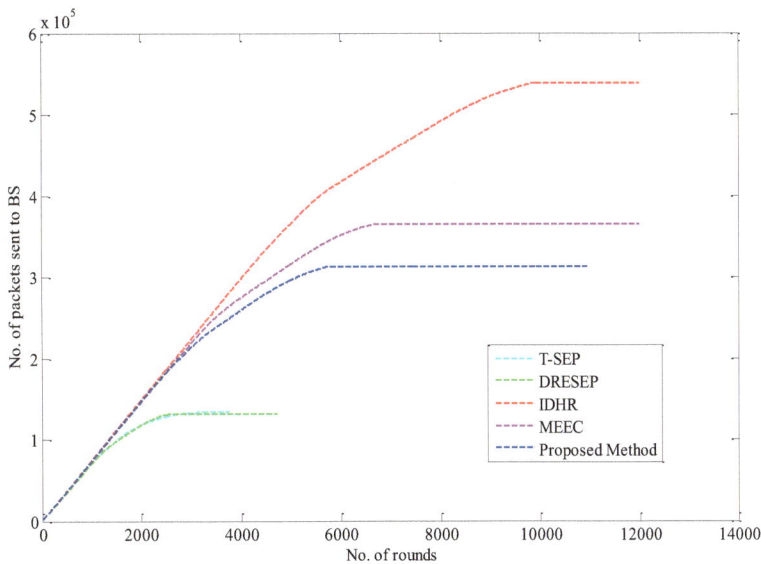

Fig. (2). Number of packets sent to BS *vs* number of rounds.

Total remaining energy: The simulation behavior of proposed approach is measured to analyze the performance of energy consumption in the form of total remaining energy. The comparative analysis per round for multiple sink is shown in Fig. (**3**). The initial energy consumption starts when CHs send an advertisement packet to BS. It is observed that the proposed approach consumes less amount of energy per round in comparison with MEEC, IDHR, DRESEP and TSEP. This improvement is due to better localization of CHs using and the best path of sink movement is selected. Here, energy consumption depends on so many factors, such as the distance of CHs to cluster members, the distance of CHs to sink, the number of CHs, *etc*. The comparative analysis shown in Fig. (**3**) illustrates that the proposed approach has shown a significant decrease in energy consumption when compared to MEEC, IDHR, DRESEP and TSEP.

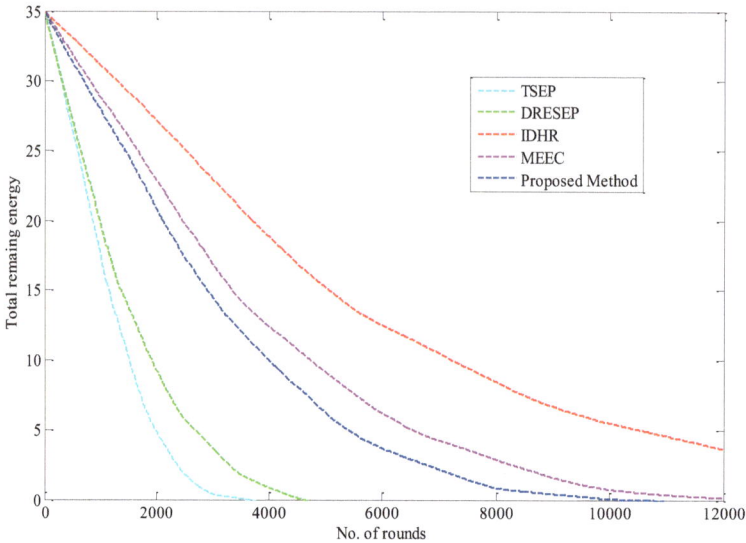

Fig. (3). Network remaining energy *vs* number of rounds.

CONCLUSION

In this chapter, the proposed work has shown the result of the mobility of the sink by considering two routing protocols IDHR and MEEC to understand the behavior of the network and simulation of the network. The threshold calculation, which is probabilistic based, is used to determine the candidates for the cluster head selection. The simulation shows better results as compared to MEEC, IDHR, DRESEP, and TSEP. It can also be observed that the more the change in position for each round, the more the network lifetime. Hence, the above analysis shows that the mobility of the sink has proved to increase the network lifetime. Moreover, the network lifetime is increased by 268%, 191%, 27%, and 17% when compared to MEEC, IDHR, DRESEP, and TSEP respectively.

This work can be extended in the future to predict the pattern of energy degradation of each node and whole network under the sink movement in single and multiple sinks. The extension can also be made in analyzing the factors that are responsible for choosing the cluster head of the network sector and also to improvise the equation for calculating the direct communication of the node with the sink, thus reducing the network degradation through the hotspot problem. This can also be extended to study and determine the best region of mobility for improved network performance and to understand the sink placement strategy in the region where human intervention is difficult.

REFERENCES

[1]   W.B. Heinzelman, A.P. Chandrakasan, and H. Balakrishnan, "An application-specific protocol architecture for wireless microsensor networks", *IEEE Trans. Wirel. Commun.,* vol. 1, no. 4, pp. 660-670, 2002.
[http://dx.doi.org/10.1109/TWC.2002.804190]

[2]   O. Younis, and S. Fahmy, "HEED: A hybrid, energy-efficient, distributed clustering approach for ad hoc sensor networks", *IEEE Trans. Mobile Comput.,* vol. 3, no. 4, pp. 366-379, 2004.
[http://dx.doi.org/10.1109/TMC.2004.41]

[3]   R. Zimmermann, "An energy-efficient voting-based clustering algorithm for sensor networks", *In Proceedings of the Sixth International Conference on Software Engineering, Artificial Intelligence, Networking and Parallell Distributed Computing and First ACIS International Workshop on Self-Assembling Wireless Networks (SNPD/SA WN 2005),* pp. 444-451, 2005.

[4]   M. Ye, C. Li, G. Chen, and J. Wu, "An energy efficient clustering scheme in wireless sensor networks", *Ad Hoc Sens. Wirel. Netw.,* vol. 3, pp. 99-119, 2007.

[5]   Z.G. Sun, Z.W. Zheng, S.J. Xu, and S.H. Chen, "Energy-aware data gathering protocol for wireless sensor networks", *3rd IEEE International Conference,* vol. 7, pp. 103-107, 2010.

[6]   S. Singh, and A. Malik, "Heterogeneous energy efficient protocol for enhancing the lifetime in WSNs", *Int. J. Inform.Technol. Comp. Sci.,* vol. 8, no. 9, pp. 62-72, 2016.
[http://dx.doi.org/10.5815/ijitcs.2016.09.08]

[7]   A.S. Nandan, S. Singh, and L.K. Awasthi, "An efficient cluster head election based on optimized genetic algorithm for movable sinks in IoT enabled HWSNs", *Appl. Soft Comput.,* vol. 107, p. 107318, 2021.
[http://dx.doi.org/10.1016/j.asoc.2021.107318]

[8]   S. Singh, A.S. Nandan, A. Malik, N. Kumar, and A. Barnawi, "An energy-efficient modified metaheuristic inspired algorithm for disaster management system using WSNs", *IEEE Sens. J.,* vol. 21, no. 13, pp. 15398-15408, 2021.
[http://dx.doi.org/10.1109/JSEN.2021.3074497]

[9]   P. Gupta, S. Tripathi, and S. Singh, "Energy efficient hotspot problem mitigation techniques using multiple mobile sink in heterogeneous wireless sensor network", *Int. J. Commun. Syst.,* vol. 33, no. 18, p. e4641, 2020.
[http://dx.doi.org/10.1002/dac.4641]

[10] S. Singh, "An energy aware clustering and data gathering technique based on nature inspired optimization in WSNs", *Peer-to-Peer Netw. Appl.,* vol. 13, no. 5, pp. 1357-1374, 2020.
[http://dx.doi.org/10.1007/s12083-020-00890-w]

[11] S. Singh, P.K. Singh, and A. Malik, "OSEP: An optimized stable election protocol in heterogeneous wireless sensor networks", *The International Conference on Recent Innovations in Computing,* pp. 235-251, 2020.

[12] A. Malik, S. Singh, and P.K. Singh, "DACHE: A data aggregation-based effective and optimized cluster head election routing protocol for HWSNs", *The International Conference on Recent Innovations in Computing,* pp. 275-292, 2020.

[13] S. Singh, *A Clustering-Based Optimized Stable Election Protocol in Wireless Sensor Networks.*

Applications in Ubiquitous Computing, 2020, pp. 157-176.

[14]   S. Singh, "A sustainable data gathering technique based on nature inspired optimization in WSNs", *Sustainable Computing: Informatics and Systems,* vol. 24, p. 100354, 2019.
[http://dx.doi.org/10.1016/j.suscom.2019.100354]

[15]   S. Singh, and A. Malik, "hetDEEC: Heterogeneous DEEC protocol for prolonging lifetime in wireless sensor networks", *J. Informa.Optimiz. Sci.,* vol. 38, no. 5, pp. 699-720, 2017.
[http://dx.doi.org/10.1080/02522667.2016.1220083]

[16]   S. Chand, S. Singh, and B. Kumar, "Heterogeneous HEED protocol for wireless sensor networks", *Wirel. Pers. Commun.,* vol. 77, no. 3, pp. 2117-2139, 2014.
[http://dx.doi.org/10.1007/s11277-014-1629-y]

[17]   A.K Sharma, N Sood, and S Verma, "A novelistic approach for energy efficient routing using single and multiple data sinks in heterogeneous wireless sensor network", *Networking and Applications,* vol. 12, pp. 1110-1136, 2019.

CHAPTER 6

IoT Based Home Security System

Manju[1,*] and **Priyanshi Pandey**[1]

¹ Department of Computer Science and Information Technology, Jaypee Institute of Information Technology, Noida, Uttar Pradesh, India

Abstract: Internet of Things (IoT)-enabled intelligent systems are proliferating rapidly, providing the capability to connect virtually any device to the Internet. Consequently, this concept can be effectively utilized in home security applications. In this paper, we have introduced an IoT-enabled system designed to send security alerts to users *via* email upon detecting human intrusion. The system comprises a PIR sensor, Pi camera, Raspberry Pi-3, and an Internet connection. There are two operational modes in the proposed security system. In the first mode, movement by an intruder is detected, and simultaneously, every time someone rings the doorbell, the Pi camera captures an image. The system then accesses a stored database to ascertain whether the individual is recognized. If the person is unfamiliar, the user receives an email notification, including the captured image of the individual. On the other hand, if the person is recognized, the system stores the captured image. In the second mode, when someone exhibits suspicious behaviour in front of the door, the system sends an alert email to the user, prompting them to activate the security alert system installed at the entrance. For face detection, we employ the Haar cascade technique. Face recognition involves two steps: feature extraction and classification. In the feature extraction phase, we compare various algorithms, and a comparative study of these provides a methodology that achieves 99.56% accuracy, outperforming other existing models. The developed system leverages the IoT platform to fortify security against intruders, thereby fostering a safe and secure environment.

Keywords: Face recognition, Home security system, Internet of things.

1. INTRODUCTION

In today's rapidly progressing world, automatic devices are increasingly replacing their manual counterparts, paving the way towards optimal and more convenient solutions. The Internet, serving as the foundation for communication, is being integrated into various devices to establish enhanced communication channels. Over the last few decades, internet usage has soared, and the field of the Internet

* **Corresponding author Manju:** Department of Computer Science and Information Technology, Jaypee Institute of Information Technology, Noida, Uttar Pradesh, India; E-mail: manju.nunia@gmail.com

Samayveer Singh , Manju, Aruna Malik, and Pradeep Kumar Singh (Eds.)

of Things (IoT) has emerged, allowing for the sharing of various kinds of information whenever needed [1, 2].

From small gadgets to entire industries, information is now at our fingertips. Every device in your home can be controlled remotely from anywhere in the world using an automated home system, providing security against theft or hazards, and creating a sense of safety and peace of mind. In this 21st-century landscape, automating home devices is becoming a norm, simplifying daily tasks and transforming living spaces. However, for home automation to reach its full potential, technological advancements are necessary, allowing for seamless communication between devices, whether wired or wireless. IoT stands out as a transformative tool in this domain, providing a pathway to a more convenient and efficient life. This paper focuses on implementing a cost-effective and easily installable IoT-based home security system, featuring a range of controls and energy-saving capabilities. Users can access and control their homes from any part of the world, enhancing their sense of security. The system allows users to log into their accounts from anywhere, monitoring entries into their homes through an application connected to the internet. The user-friendly interface of the proposed system ensures accessibility for anyone with an internet connection. Additionally, the system's affordability sets it apart from similar products in the market. Our system ensures rapid response to any kind of intrusion, allowing users to access and monitor their desired location using just an internet connection and a device. It employs two main approaches: face detection and face recognition [3, 4]. These tasks, however, are challenging due to the variety of factors that must be considered. To address this, we explore various algorithms, identifying the three most promising approaches: pre-trained convolutional neural networks (ResNet-50 and VGG-16), and the Local Binary Pattern Histogram (LBPH) algorithm. Haar cascade is used for its efficiency in face detection, and the Support Vector Machine (SVM) algorithm for classification. Despite its advantages, the system is not without limitations. Giving access to unauthorized individuals through the system is akin to handing over your house keys, a risk present in traditional systems as well. Nevertheless, when compared to other security systems, such as fingerprint or house ID-based systems, our solution offers a more optimal approach. Various algorithms were compared based on speed, accuracy, and space requirements to identify the best possible solution. The proposed system includes a webcam for facial image recognition, and cross-referencing with stored images in a database. If face recognition is successful, the door unlocks, the user receives an email with an image of the visitor, and the information is saved in the database. In the case of an intruder, the door remains locked, and the homeowner is immediately notified *via* email. The Raspberry Pi 4 serves as the main controller of the system, with the Face Recognition (FR) system validating identities against a database and employing the OpenCV library for image processing. The system's camera module, together with the haar cascade classifier for face detection and SVM algorithm for face recognition, ensures accurate and reliable security measures [5].

2. RELATED WORK

Face detection and face recognition are crucial parameters for home security systems, requiring 24-hour surveillance, cost-effectiveness, and the highest possible accuracy. In this section, we have discussed various models based on these parameters and conducted a comparative study to analyze their challenges, with the aim of developing a model that maximizes accuracy while maintaining cost-effectiveness and low time and space complexity.

One of the studies [6] presents a comparative study of two different face recognition models, utilized to build a home security system capable of detecting the presence of an intruder and alerting the user. The Viola-Jones method has been employed for face detection, while Independent Component Analysis (ICA) and Principal Component Analysis (PCA) have been considered for face recognition. Photos of intruders are taken as soon as they enter, and these are subsequently sent to the system for comparison with a database of authorized individuals. The two models, ICA and PCA, yield accuracy rates of 86.7% and 76.7%, respectively, leading to the conclusion that the ICA algorithm surpasses the PCA algorithm in terms of accuracy.

The CNN [7] method, known for its high accuracy in face recognition, has been implemented in a home security system. A database consisting of a number of 1048 images of user faces has been used to train the model, employing the AlexNet convolutional neural network, which comprises eight layers. The results indicate an accuracy rate of 97.5%.

Home security is a paramount concern, and the system proposed in [8] addresses this issue through the use of IoT, training a model to perform face detection and recognition. The system compares images from an existing database with captured images to determine whether an individual is authorized to enter. This automated system is cost-effective, consumes low power, and its efficiency is enhanced by IoT, making it suitable for real-time applications. It achieves an approximate accuracy of 95% and enables remote monitoring of the house over a Wide Area Network (WAN).

The trend of smart homes is escalating daily, with increasing numbers of people opting for automated security systems for convenience and safety. According to a 2022 survey report [9], over 500 smart devices are in use by families, offering convenience and ease of use. Smart devices, supported by continuous technological advancements, significantly simplify life and lead to the development of new applications.

In the work proposed in [10], a model for face detection and recognition has been developed for security systems, utilizing the Local Binary Pattern Histogram (LBPH) for recognition, and trained with images stored in the database. The recognition rate may vary depending on the number of images in the database and may be adversely affected by noisy images. This versatile system can be adapted for various applications, ranging from private sectors such as malls and shops, to national security sectors. Alternatively, Aadhar or PAN cards could be used in the dataset, rather than capturing images of everyone entering a restricted area. Further enhancements to the system's efficiency can be made according to specific requirements. Additionally, the system can detect objects carried by individuals entering a private area, determining whether they pose a threat. This system has the potential to be effectively utilized as a home security system.

In the model proposed in this paper [11], as illustrated in Fig. (1), the IoT devices are connected to the cloud network through the application layer, mediated by the Application Layer Gateway (ALG).

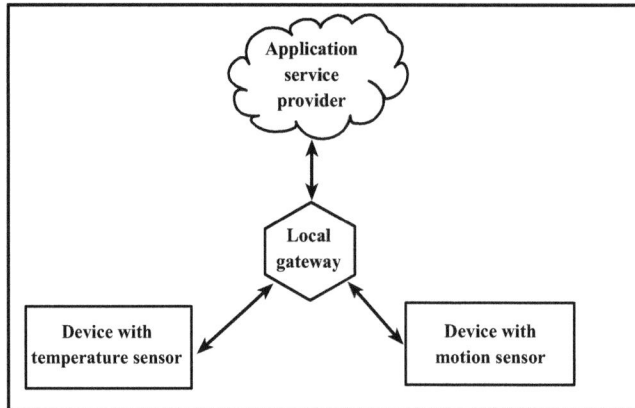

Fig. (1). Device to gate way communication.

This type of model is integrated into numerous devices currently in use. To facilitate communication between devices through relay *via* cloud networking, which users operate on their smartphone applications, the Application Layer Gateway (ALG) functions as the user's smartphone. It serves as the intermediary communication source between IoT devices and the cloud network, typically in the form of a local software application. This is necessary for devices that are unable to establish a direct communication gateway with the cloud network and require some form of mediator, such as an auxiliary source or an application. For example, a smart home application requires a gateway to facilitate communication between the IoT device and the cloud network.

Security and reliability are of paramount concern in the field of IoT [12]. Ensuring the security of the IoT system poses a significant challenge and remains a top priority for vendors. With the increasing ubiquity of internet-connected devices, the security of IoT devices is crucial; if compromised, they could be easily infiltrated by intruders, potentially harming users, leading to various forms of cybercrime, causing system malfunctions, and compromising reliability.

In the model proposed in this paper [12], as depicted in Fig. (**2**), IoT devices are connected to the cloud network for information exchange purposes, using wired Ethernet as a mediator between the IoT device and the cloud. This communication model is employed by various consumer IoT devices, such as the Nest Learning Thermostat. In this example, the thermostat, which is used to maintain a set temperature, sends data over the internet to the cloud, utilizing this data to analyze energy usage in the user's home. Additionally, users can access and review this thermostat data *via* the application. However, a limitation in this context is that only hardware and cloud services provided by the same manufacturer are compatible.

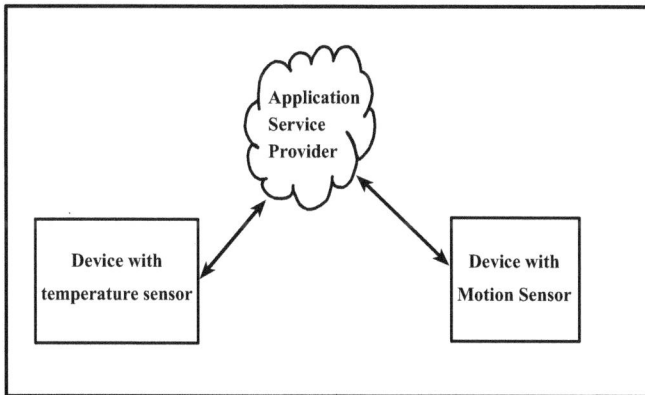

Fig. (2). Device to cloud communication.

3. PROPOSED SYSTEM ARCHITECTURE

The proposed system is designed to detect any kind of intrusion and determine whether the person entering is authorized or not. It is based primarily on two approaches: face detection and face recognition. Detecting and identifying faces is a challenging task, especially when considering all the relevant factors. To address this, various algorithms exist, and we have selected a few for consideration in order to find the best possible approach. The three approaches that will be discussed further are the pre-trained convolutional neural networks (ResNet-50 and VGG-16) and the LBPH (Local Binary Patterns Histograms) algorithm. Human faces are detected using the Haar Cascade classifier due to its various advantageous features, such as reduced time complexity and high accuracy. Following this, classification is performed with the help of the SVM (Support Vector Machine) algorithm. Therefore, we have compared various algorithms based on speed, accuracy, and space to achieve the best possible approach.

The system is implemented on a Raspberry Pi-3 because it can process captured images with low power consumption and high processing speed. The Raspberry Pi-3 comes equipped with all the vital components necessary for this system, including a camera, sensor, and various other components crucial for a home security system. In this section, we have discussed the architecture of the home security system approach as illustrated in Fig. (3). In the home security architecture, a PIR sensor is used to detect the presence of someone, and it also works in darkness. A Pi Camera is utilized to capture the image of an intruder when their presence is detected. It operates in two modes.

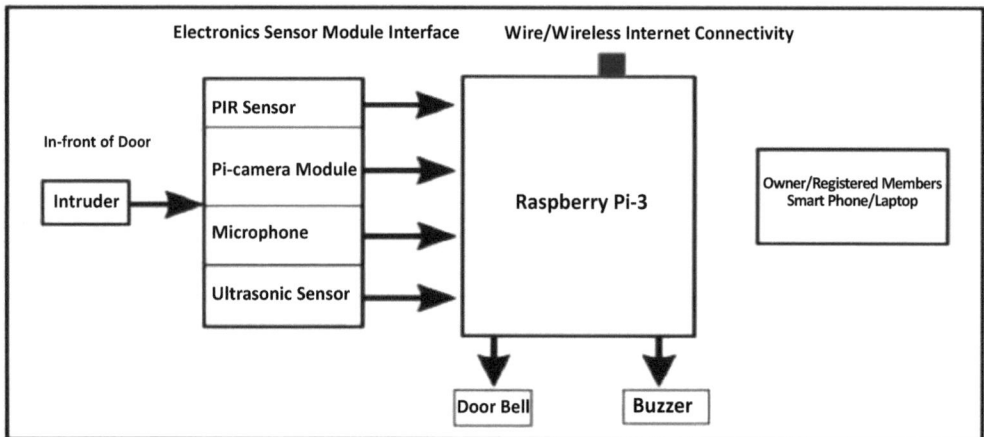

Fig. (3). System architecture.

In the first mode, if a person presses the bell button and any kind of movement is detected with the help of the sensor, the system will capture an image and save it to the database. The Raspberry Pi processes the image to identify any intruders, and then, with the help of the stored database, the system determines if the person is authorized or unauthorized. The user will be alerted *via* email if someone unauthorized is detected, with the image of that person attached to the email. Access will be granted if the person is authorized.

4. SYSTEM COMPONENTS

The various electronic components that will be used in the proposed system are discussed below:

A. Raspberry Pi 3: Model B+ The main computing device is Raspberry Pi 3 (Fig. **4**). It acquires signals from sensors, processes the signals, and sends an Intruder image to the user *via* email after processing. It captures the image using a pi camera and sends it to the system for further comparison with the existing database and also to the user *via* email.

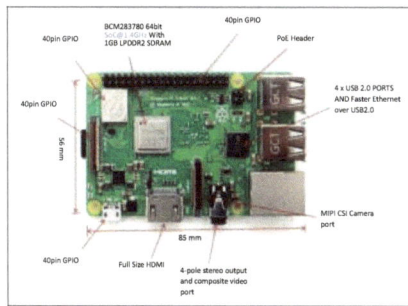

Fig. (4). Raspberry Pi 3 model B+ module.

B. Pi Camera: Pi camera (Fig. **5**) is used to capture the images and videos of any intruder in front of the home and sends it to the database to perform the proposed algorithm and allow access to the house on the basis of that.

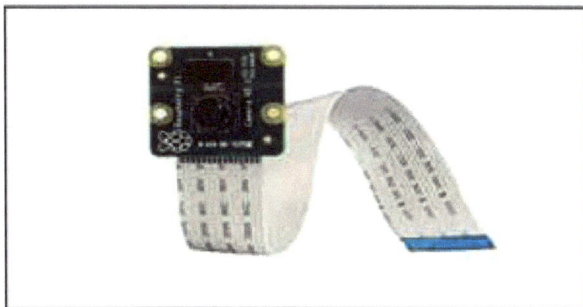

Fig. (5). Pi camera.

C. PIR Sensor (Passive Infrared Sensor): It is shown in Fig. (**6**). It measures infrared lights transmitted over the sensor range by the object for movement detection. It also works in darkness. It will help in detecting any kind of movement near the user's home and if it detects some kind of motion the Pi camera will capture the images and save them in the database.

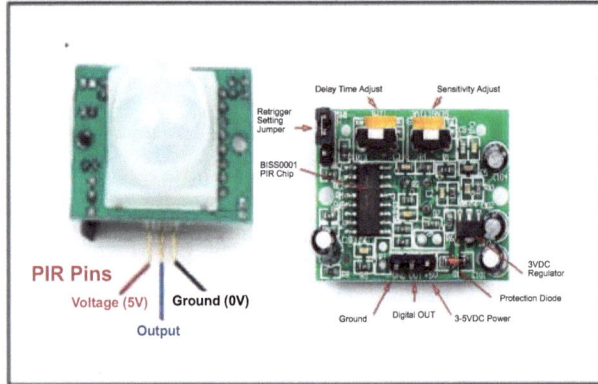

Fig. (6). PIR sensor.

In this section, we have discussed various devices that will be part of our proposed system for intruder detection at the user house. With the help of a PIR sensor, the presence of someone will be detected, and capture the images with the help of that person and *via* will send *via* email to the user. By using the defined model it will check whether the person is authorized or not, and allow the entry on the basis of that and store its information in the database with the current timestamp (Fig. **7**).

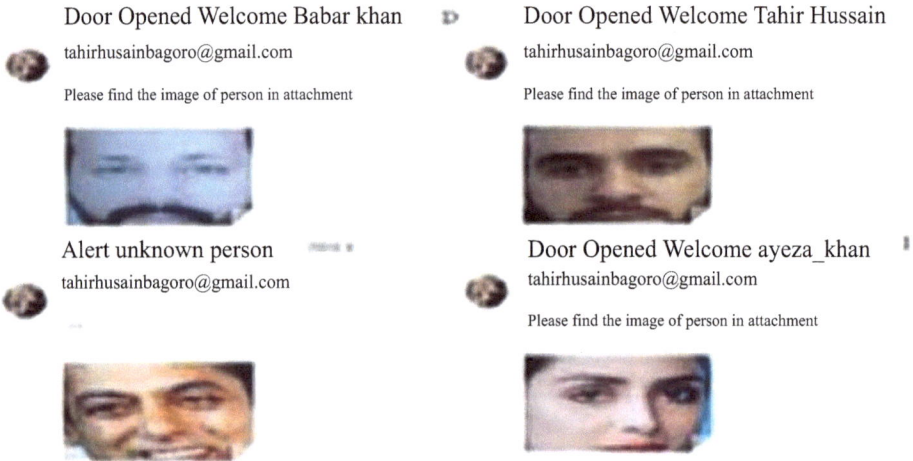

Fig. (7). Email notification.

5. SYSTEM WORKFLOW

This proposed system is utilized for the detection of intruders near the user's home. Once the presence of an intruder or any kind of movement is detected with the help of a Pi sensor, the Pi camera will commence capturing images and video. The Haar cascade technique is employed for face detection, whereas face recognition involves two steps: first, feature extraction, and second, classification. To perform feature extraction, various algorithms are compared, and the one yielding the highest accuracy will be implemented. The SVM algorithm is subsequently used for classification purposes. Using the registered email address of the user, the system will send the person's details as an attachment. Meanwhile, the captured images will be saved at the backend with the current timestamp. Only these captured images, videos, and audio will be available in the database. Then, the system will operate in two modes, depending entirely on the presence or absence of the user. Further, if the user is present, it will depend on whether the doorbell is pressed by the intruder. The system will compare this information with the database and decide whether or not this person has access to the house. These modes are discussed further in Table **1**.

Table 1. System workflow.

MODE-A (When the user is at home)		MODE-B (When the user is not at home)
If doorbell is PRESSED by the intruder	If doorbell is NOT PRESSED by the intruder	If any suspicious movement is observed at entrance/door
The captured image will be compared with data base.	The captured image will be compared with data base.	The captured image will be compared with data base.
If captured image is as per data base.	a) If captured image is as per data base, then notification will be given to owner and registered members. b) If captured image is not as per data base *i.e.* new image found, then notification will be given to owner and registered members. Alert alarm will be activated.	a) If captured image is as per data base, then notification will be given to owner and registered members. However, no alarm will be activated. b) If captured image is not as per data base *i.e.* new image found, then notification will be given to owner and registered members. Alert alarm will be activated.
No alert alarm will be activated and door can be opened.	Door can be opened by the person available at home as per notification.	

The proposed system is embedded with other core modules whose function is to send the detected images of the intruder to the user *via* email. This system uses a simple mail transfer protocol (SMTP) to notify the user about intruders. The email with attached intruder images is transferred to the user *via* this protocol and saves the person's image with the timestamp and name of the person as authorised or unauthorized in the database.

6. FACE DETECTION

Face detection plays a crucial role in applications that involve recognizing faces. This function automatically identifies faces within an image [13]. Its primary objective is to locate and recognize the human face, regardless of varying parameters such as size, brightness, or position. While this task is straightforward for humans, it presents complexities from a computer's perspective. Achieving high accuracy requires training the system on certain factors, simplifying the task, and enabling the system to distinguish between facial areas and other regions. To facilitate the recognition of human faces by the system, specific thresholds must be established. Depending on whether an image meets a particular threshold, the system determines whether the recognized image represents a face [14].

The algorithms for face detection can be categorized into two types:

Feature-Based: This algorithm detects the basic features of the human face, independent of any other factors.

Learning-Based: This category employs machine learning algorithms to train the model.

In this context, we will utilize the Viola-Jones algorithm. Although numerous algorithms exist for face detection, the Viola-Jones algorithm is renowned for its effectiveness in distinguishing faces from images. The face recognition algorithm differentiates human faces from non-human faces. Images captured by the Pi camera undergo analysis using the proposed algorithm to identify sub-windows where faces might be located. A common image processing practice involves running the detector at a fixed length after rescaling the image to a certain desired size. However, this approach can increase computation time as the system needs to be trained for variable sizes. In contrast, the proposed algorithm opts to extract the input image and run it repeatedly for all variable sizes, ensuring continuous updates. While this method may appear time-consuming due to the necessity of running the algorithm periodically, it results in a scale-invariant detector requiring a consistent number of computations, regardless of length. This detector employs simple rectangular features and Haar wavelet-transformed images. The Viola-Jones algorithm is capable of detecting human faces in images, as illustrated in Fig. (8). A dataset containing various images is provided to the system to identify the facial areas of humans. During the training phase, the system detects faces, forwards the images for pre-processing, and subsequently utilizes them for recognition and classification purposes. All features associated with the face images are compiled and stored in a file during this phase.

```
┌─────────────────┐      ┌─────────────────┐      ┌─────────────────┐
│                 │      │  B. Haar Like   │      │                 │
│  A. Face Image  │ ───▶ │    Feature      │ ───▶ │ C. Integral Image│
│                 │      │                 │      │                 │
└─────────────────┘      └─────────────────┘      └─────────────────┘
                                                            │
                                                            ▼
                         ┌─────────────────┐      ┌─────────────────┐
                         │  E.Cascade of   │      │  D. Adaptive    │
                         │   Classifier    │ ◀─── │  Boosting or    │
                         │                 │      │   AdaBoost      │
                         └─────────────────┘      └─────────────────┘
```

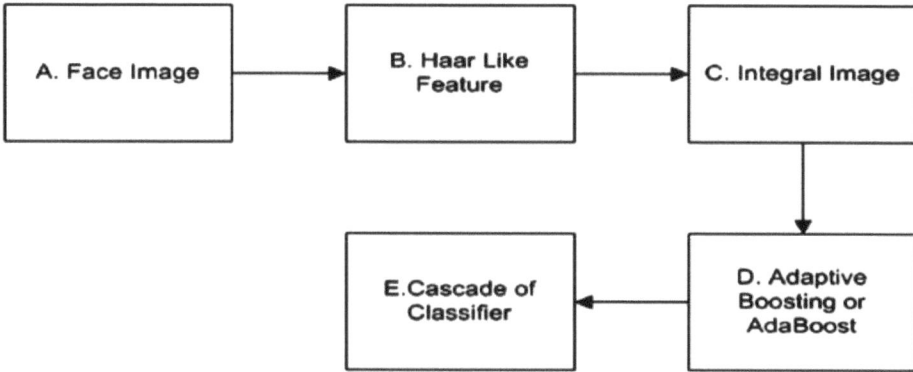

Fig. (8). Face detection.

The next phase after training the data set is the testing phase. During the test phase, for the classification of the image (face or non-face) the stored features are used. If all thresholds are exceeded by the input image, it is classified as a face and if it does not then it is denoted non-face. The Viol-Jones algorithm can be divided into four steps, these are:

Haar feature selection:

There are certain properties all human faces share, by using Haar features these similarities can be matched. There are also some features that can show irregularities, it can be differences in the shade of upper checks and eye area or the area of the nose bridge, which all have variation in complexion. The similarities that the human face share can be the location of facial features.

An integral image:

In the second step of this algorithm for face detection, the input image is rotated into an integral image. Every pixel is created comparable to the total sum of all the pixels that are above it or on the left side of that pixel. This results in a specific rectangle by the use of only four values by computing the sum of all the pixels.

Adaboost training:

The suggested algorithm has a base window of size 24x24 for the evaluation of all the features that exist in the given image. If all the Haar features parameters are considered, then that will result in evaluating 160000+ features in the allotted window. However, this algorithm only evaluates prominent features in any input image with a 24x24 window. All the useless features that are repetitive are eradicated and only useful ones are analysed, and for the selection of those features that are useful, Adaboost is used. It basically gets rid of all the features that are not important and repetitive. This is the part that causes maximum time latency as the only way is the brute force method but simplifies the training process and makes the system faster and more efficient.

Cascading classifier:

The collection of all the strong classifiers is known as a cascaded classifier. The purpose of all the previous phases was verification on the basis of whether it is a face or not in the particular sub-window. The sub-window will be discarded if it is classified as non-face, otherwise, in the case of maybe face image, the sub-window continues to the next phase in the cascade. The probability of the sub-window is being classified as a face increase.

7. FACE RECOGNITION

The Face Recognition model role is basically the identification of a person on the basis of a comparison of input images that are stored in the database. Usually, face recognition can be further divided into three stages: detection, extraction, and recognition. Face detection detects the human face in any input image, but the accuracy rate can change due to several factors in the process of face detection and face recognition, those six factors are:

The images that are been classified will be stored in the existing database as shown in Fig. (**9**). To implement this system, we have used Raspberry Pi as it iscost-effective and efficient.

8. RESULT AND DISCUSSION

This section discusses the results we achieved by implementing the proposed model. This system primarily relies on two approaches: face detection and face recognition. Detecting and identifying faces is a challenging task, especially when all relevant factors are taken into consideration. To perform this task, various algorithms exist.

We have considered some of these algorithms to find the best possible approach. All the other existing models have an accuracy rate of less than 90%, while the accuracy rates achieved by the ResNet-50, VGG-16, and LBPH algorithms are more than 90%, specifically 99.56%, 98.49%, and 98.47%, respectively.

Table **2** represents the training time for each model, although the LBPH algorithm takes the least amount of time, however, the accuracy rate of ResNet-50 is comparatively better than the two other algorithms.

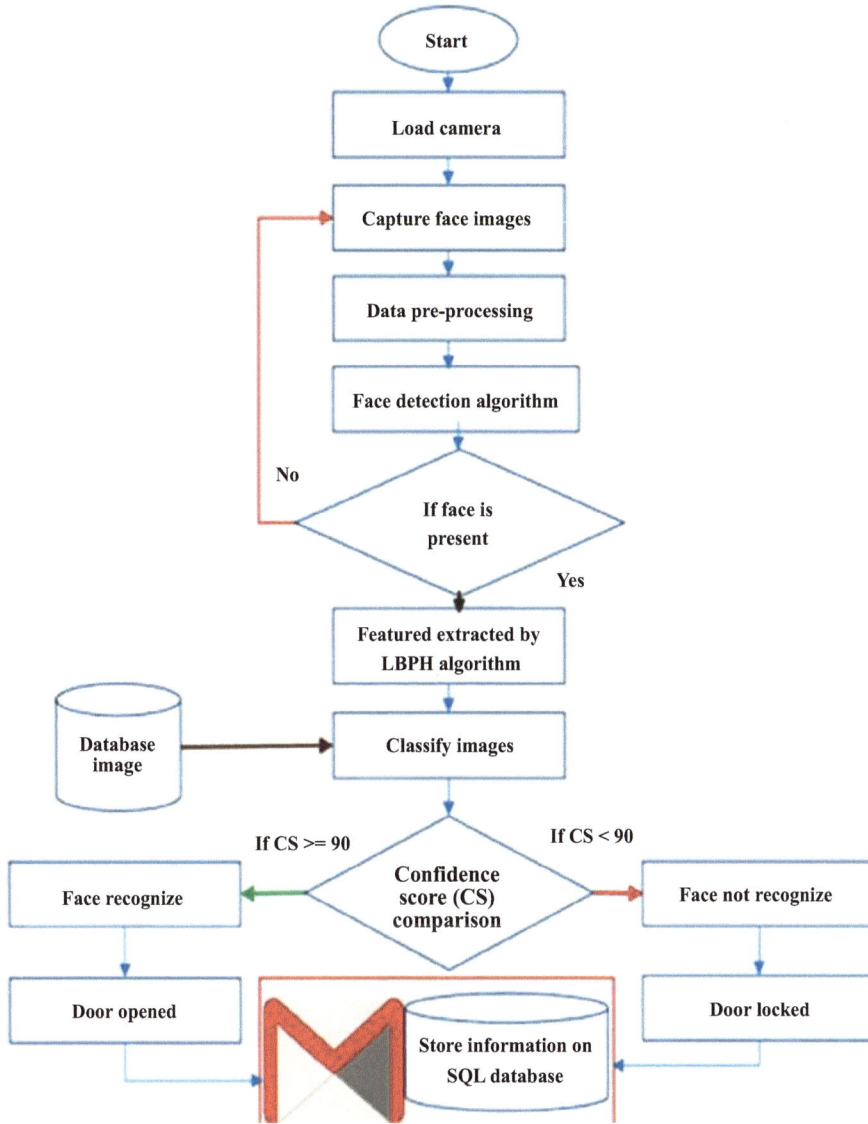

Fig. (9). System workflow.

Table 2. Training time.

Method	Training Time	Accuracy
ResNet-50	1.205 hours	99.56%
VGG-16	1.346 hours	98.49%
LBPH	0.189 hours	98.47%

CONCLUSION AND FUTURE WORK

In this proposed system, an automatic facial recognition system for home security has been successfully implemented using a Raspberry Pi 3 Model B+. Users are able to receive notifications *via* email on their smartphones and laptops anytime and anywhere. In the event that any suspicious movement is detected, the built-in alarm system will be triggered, and an email containing an image of the intruder will be sent to the user, with the image also being saved in the database. As a result, the proposed system prevents access by any unwanted individuals, overcoming the drawbacks of all existing automated or traditional systems such as keys, patterns, and passwords. Due to its lower power consumption, smaller size, and lighter weight, we have chosen to implement this system using a Raspberry Pi instead of a PC-based system, as it is more convenient. The system recognizes both known and unknown individuals based on the images stored in the database and also sends the user an image of any intruder *via* email using the SMTP protocol. The use of Raspberry Pi modules offers ample opportunities for enhancements in performance. Detecting and identifying faces is a challenging task, especially when taking all relevant factors into consideration. To address this, various algorithms exist, and we have selected a few for consideration in order to find the best possible approach. The three approaches that will be discussed further are pre-trained convolutional neural networks (ResNet-50 and VGG-16), and the LBPH (Local Binary Patterns Histograms) algorithm. Human faces are detected using the Haar Cascade classifier due to its various advantageous features, such as reduced time complexity and high accuracy, and then classification is performed with the help of the Support Vector Machine (SVM) algorithm.

In the future, IoT-based security systems could be employed in banking systems, retail settings, and private businesses, and for securing debit cards to prevent fraud. Additionally, there is potential for the system to be integrated and synchronized with local police department databases for the purpose of identifying and monitoring criminals.

REFERENCES

[1]   R. Kishore, V. Jain, S. Bose, and L. Boppana, "IoT based smart security and home automation system", *2016 International Conference on Computing. International Conference on Computing, Communication and Automation (ICCCA)*, 2016.

[2]   O.M. Parkhi, A. Vedaldi, and A. Zisserman, "Deep face recognition", In: *Proceedings of the British Machine Vision Conference (BMVC)*, X. Xie, M. W. Jones, G. K. L. Tam, Eds., BMVA Press, 2015.

[3]   D.A. Waatti, "Design of face detaction and recognition system for smart home security application", *In: 2017 2nd Intarnational confarences on Informetion Technalogy, Information Systems and Electrical Engineering*, pp. 342-347, 2017.

[4]   M. Waseem, S.A. Khowaja, R.K. Ayyasamy, and F. Bashir, "Face recognition for smart door lock

system using hierarchical network", *2020 International Conference on Computational Intelligence (ICCI)*, Bandar Seri Iskandar, Malaysia, pp.51-56, 2020.
[http://dx.doi.org/10.1109/ICCI51257.2020.9247836]

[5]   Y. Zhang, and L. Wu, "Classification of fruits using computer vision and a multiclass support vector machine", *Sensors*, vol. 12, no. 9, pp. 12489-12505, 2012.
[http://dx.doi.org/10.3390/s120912489] [PMID: 23112727]

[6]   D.A. Chowdhry, A. Hussain, M.Z. Ur Rehman, F. Ahmad, A. Ahmad, and M. Pervaiz, "Smart security system for sensitive area using face recognition", *2013 IEEE Conference on Sustainable Utilization and Development in Engineering and Technology (CSUDET)*, pp.11-14, 2013.
[http://dx.doi.org/10.1109/CSUDET.2013.6670976]

[7]   N.S. Irnto, and N. Surntha, "Home security system with face recognition based on convlutional neurel network", *Int. J. Adv. Comput. Sci. Appl.*, vol. 11, no. 11, 2020.

[8]   Sana Ghafor, Dr Khatak, and Mustfa Taher, "Home automotion security systam based on face detection and recagnition using IoT", *In book: Intelligent Technologies and Applications*, 2020.

[9]   Margeratt Rose, Website definition, Last updated in 2005(Tech Target), Accessed on: September 6, 2015.

[10]   R. Manjunatha1, and Dr. R. Nageraja, "Home security system and door acess control based on face recogntion", *Int. Res. J. Eng. Technol*, vol. 4, no. 3, 2017.

[11]   Mescha Dohlar, "Mechine to machine technolgies", 2013.

[12]   J.N. Al-Karaki, K-C. Chen, G. Morabito, and J. Oliveira, "From M2M communications to the internet of things: Opportunities and challenges", *Ad Hoc Netw.*, vol. 18, pp. 1-2, 2014.
[http://dx.doi.org/10.1016/j.adhoc.2014.03.006]

[13]   J. Ruen, and J. Yen, "Face datection based on faciel features and lineer support vector machines", *Proc. 2009 International Conference on Communication Software and Networks* Macau, China, pp.371-375, 2009.
[http://dx.doi.org/10.1109/ICCSN.2009.76]

[14]   C. Güre, and A. Erden, "Design of a face recognition system", *The 15th International Conference on Machine Design and Production*, UMTIK 2012.

CHAPTER 7

Cyber Security from a Business Perspective

Vikas Verma[1], Amit Garg[2] and Saurabh Singhal[3,*]

[1] *iNurture, Teerthanker Mahaveer University, Moradabad, Uttar Pradesh, India*

[2] *Department of Computer Science, Manipal University, Jaipur, India*

[3] *Department of Computer Science and Engineering, Apex Institute of Technology, Chandigarh University, Chandigarh, India*

Abstract: In today's era of Information Technology, we have encountered drastic changes in computing methodologies due to a tremendous increase in ONLINE communication traffic both in terms of the number of users and data communication. The COVID–19 pandemic has brought the entire world online. Cyber Security plays an important role in the field of information technology. In order to secure information, one can face many challenges. Nowadays, governments and other organisations are following various measures to prevent vivid cybercrimes. In this chapter, we have raised concern over the drastic increment in an ONLINE communication system, which urges the need for the development and deployment of Cyber Security in a business environment.

Keywords: Business resilience, Cloud computing, Data breach, Internet of things.

1. INTRODUCTION

The transition of the entire education system to an online format has rendered the situation increasingly catastrophic. Taking into account the current trends in online communication, we have been analyzing and progressing at a defined pace. However, the current situation presents a significant challenge that we are struggling to cope with. This sudden shift in the behavior of data transmission has catapulted us approximately 10 years forward, forcing us to adapt to a communication system that is not deemed suitable for meeting these abrupt demands [1]. The one-minute intervals over the last three years on the Internet illustrate the surge in online communication.

The graph depicted in Fig. **(1)** highlights the growth in the number of Google users accessing the Internet per minute. In 2017, the count stood at 3.5 million users; it increased to 3.7 million in 2018, 3.8 million in 2019, and reached 4.7 mil-

---

* **Corresponding author Saurabh Singhal:** Department of Computer Science and Engineering, Apex Institute of Technology, Chandigarh University, Chandigarh, India; E-mail: saurabh.singhal09@gmail.com

Samayveer Singh , Manju, Aruna Malik, and Pradeep Kumar Singh (Eds.)

lion by 2020. Examining the rate of increase showcased in Fig. (**2**), the year 2019-2020 witnessed an almost fivefold surge compared to earlier periods. Observing these trends, our IT sector has progressively shifted towards embracing the latest in computing innovations, undergoing significant transformations from Cloud Computing to IoT, then to Cloud IoT, and eventually to Fog Computing.

No. of Google Users in One Minute

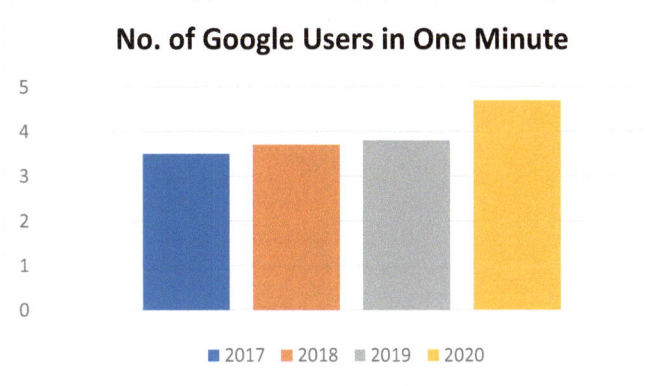

Fig. (1). Number of Google users in one minute over the years.

Rate of Increment

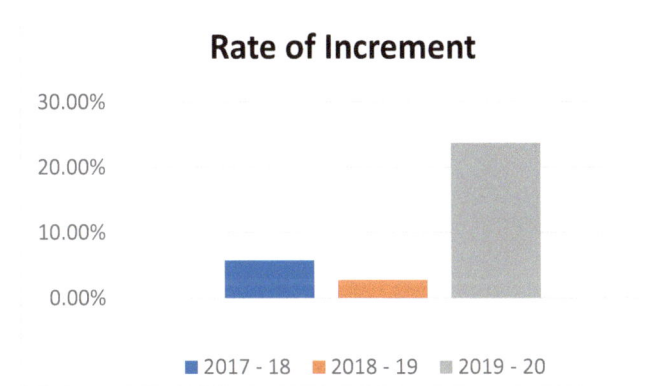

Fig. (2). Rate of increase in the number of Google users.

Before moving further, let us discuss these terms:

- **Cloud Computing** – Cloud computing is defined as the online delivery of various software and hardware services *via* the Internet. These resources encompass high-computing servers, data storage, networking, databases, and software [2]. Rather than storing data on a personal hard drive or local storage device, cloud-based storage enables saving it to a remote database. As a result, data can be accessed from anywhere, provided there is an electronic device with

Internet connectivity. Nowadays, users manage vast amounts of data due to the proliferation of numerous IoT devices. Consequently, cloud computing has become a preferred option for individuals and businesses alike, offering benefits such as cost savings, increased productivity, speed, efficiency, performance, and security [3].

- **IoT** – The Internet of Things (IoT) refers to a network of interconnected computing devices, mechanical and digital machines, objects, animals, or people, each provided with unique identifiers (UIDs). These entities have the capability to transfer data over a network without the necessity for human-t--human or human-to-computer interaction [4]. In the realm of IoT, a "thing" could be a person with a heart monitor implant, a farm animal equipped with a biochip transponder, an automobile outfitted with sensors to alert the driver of low tire pressure or any other natural or man-made object that can be assigned an Internet Protocol (IP) address and capable of transmitting data over a network [9, 10].

- **CloudIoT** – An IoT cloud constitutes an extensive network that supports IoT devices and applications, incorporating the requisite infrastructure, servers, and storage necessary for real-time operations and processing. Examples include Amazon Web Services IoT, IBM Watson IoT Platform, and Microsoft Azure IoT Hub.

These transitions have led us to encounter unexpected and challenging situations regarding implementation, due to the unique characteristics and behaviors specific to each methodology. Nevertheless, we have managed to cope with these circumstantial challenges using our knowledge and intelligence, striving to implement advancements in computing methodologies to prevent such issues from arising in the future. According to INFOGIX trends around 2017, there has been an amalgamation of Big Data, IoT, and Cloud Computing. Implementing any one of these technologies is not possible without interacting with the domains of the others. They are closely and strongly interconnected, along with their sub-dimensions. However, when implementing any computing methodology, another major concern and aspect that we must consider is the Security Aspect.

The Security Aspect encompasses mechanisms related to all dimensions of the IT sector, including physical, hardware, software, firmware, network, application, and any other dimensions that one might consider. Expert professionals have consolidated these dimensions under the term "CYBER SECURITY". The term "CYBER" covers all aspects related to computing, computing devices, and Internet communication. In brief, we can assert that cyber security can be implemented in any scenario if we successfully apply the principles of the CIA Triad – Confidentiality, Integrity, and Availability. We must also be mindful of implementing the Principles of Information Assurance, which provide assurance that the communication system we have adopted is secure and safe, instilling a sense of security as a result of implementing Cyber Security.

Our main focus is on ensuring that in a communication system with multiple stages and End-to-End devices, where large amounts of data are transferred due to the involvement of vital IoT devices, communication protocols, and other security mechanisms play a crucial role in maintaining security. We are confident that our communication is fully secure; however, we find it challenging to identify security issues at the sender or receiver ends since current cybersecurity concepts do not address this scenario. Nowadays, fog computing is being implemented to manage such scenarios effectively.

2. BEST PRACTICES FOR IMPLEMENTING BUSINESS RESILIENCE DURING A DATA BREACH

Business resilience is regarded as the capacity of an organization to swiftly adjust to unforeseen circumstances during the execution of business operations, ensuring the protection of assets, and personnel, and the maintenance of its global reputation. It goes a step beyond disaster recovery by offering post-disaster strategies to prevent downtime, address vulnerabilities, and manage business operations amidst unexpected breaches. This process requires a comprehensive understanding of workflows, meticulously designed to withstand unforeseen events. A frequently underestimated challenge in this realm is the human element; it is crucial to train individuals effectively, enabling them to respond appropriately in specific chaotic situations. (Fig. **3**).

1 BUSINESS CONTINUITY	2 CRISIS MANAGE-MENT	3 CRISIS RESPONSE	4 IT SERVICE CONTINUITY	5 TESTING, SIMULATION, EDUCATION
BUSINESS MODEL	**ACTING IN CRISIS**	**PREPARE AND REACT**	**DIGITAL RESILIENCE**	**PEOPLE**
• Crisis Scenarios • Business Impact • Emergency Planning • Policies and Governance • Resilient Business Model • Digitally Transformed	• Crisis Management • Crisis Organization • Crisis Communication	• Crisis Planning • Crisis Preparation • Continuous controls for status of preparedness • Partner network for crisis situations • Supply chain preparedness and continuity	• Business and IT Alignment • Cyber Risk and Impact Analysis • Building Cyber Resilience • Fallback planning for IT outages, WFH scenarios etc. • C-SCRM	• Test plans • Simulate crisis and its impacts • Educate teams • Gather ideas for continuous improvement

Fig. (3). Best practices for implementing business resilience during a data breach.

Business resilience embodies the ability to rapidly adapt to risks and disruptions, all while preserving crucial business workflows, and safeguarding employees, assets, and brand reputation. The management of business resilience is paramount for ensuring the survival of a business in the face of constantly evolving IT landscapes, cyber threats, and regulatory environments.

A data breach is referred to as an event where information has been stolen from a computer system without the knowledge of the Computer System's owner or authorization. Organizations whether small or big may suffer from data breach. Data that is being stolen may be sensitive, proprietary, or confidential (like Customer Data, Trade secrets, Matters of National Security, *etc.*). Data Breach may result in the form of damage to the reputation of the targeted company due to "betrayal of trust" [5]. The targeted company may also suffer from financial loss.

2.1. Practices for Implementing Business Resilience

(1). Act Promptly –A data breach requires immediate action from the organization. We have to identify the location where the vulnerability exists and implement a disaster recovery plan. We can make it more prompt by performing regular testing.

(2). Act openly – It requires quick acceptance from an individual or an organization so that remedial measures can be implemented as soon as possible. Because if we are unable to inform people in a prescribed time frame then it will lead us to suffer from losses in terms of finances and reputation as well.

(3). Identification of Issue – We can find flaws in our network communication system and must try to identify the reasons for the occurrence of the said breach *i.e.*, the reason for vulnerability and how to overcome it. Further, we try to investigate other possible reasons like Human Error or Fault in our Process Workflow.

(4). Predicting future attacks – We always believe that prevention is better than cure. We should implement a practice of continuous monitoring of risks and their control measures. While implementing social engineering we have to conduct physical and logical penetration testing regularly to strengthen the organization's susceptibility. Also, implementing such practices at vendors or clients ends [6].

(5). Encounter the Unforeseen – Nowadays, incidents related to Data breaches are becoming common and an organization's efficiency is being measured over the capability to face such unforeseen circumstances. The more efficient the organization is the more value in the market is. So, we have to plan our policies in such a way that we can adapt countermeasures and safeguards at runtime to meet the unseen events and actions. Our system must be prompt and always ready to act wisely against these ill practices prevailing in the current scenario.

2.2. Checklist for Implementing Business Resilience during Data Breach

(1). Create the Team – Implementing a BCP plan unquestionably requires a committed group. Groups ought to be worked in view of pecking order, with explicit jobs and recuperation errands doled out to staff individuals who are responsible for each.

(2). Drawing Business Continuity Plan – Mapping out a methodology is perhaps the main part of a business coherence plan. The destinations of the arrangement ought to be unmistakably perceived with objectives set appropriately. An organization should utilize this chance to distinguish the key cycles and individuals who will keep it running.

To draw up the arrangement, organizations need to make a rundown of the relative multitude of interruptions that could influence an organization's tasks. Pinpoint basic capacities in regular business measures and define reasonable recuperation systems for every conceivable debacle situation.

(3). Perform Business Impact Analysis – After distinguishing all the expected dangers, they ought to be altogether examined. An appropriate business sway investigation or BIA ought to be set up. Broad records may be readied, contingent upon the organization's setup and topographical area.

The rundown can incorporate floods, tropical storms, fires, volcanoes, and even Tsunamis. Aside from the above cataclysmic events, others have a lot higher likelihood of happening. These can incorporate cyber-attacks, vacations because of blackouts, information debasement, framework disappointments, equipment shortcomings, and other noxious dangers to information security.

(4). Instructions and Training – Handling business progression requires information past that of IT experts and those with network safety capability. Organizations at the upper administration level need to design the targets, necessities, and key segments of the arrangement before the entire group. Build up an extensive preparation system to assist the group with building up the necessary abilities.

(5). Identification of Sensitive Information – Every business works with basic information dispensed with the highest security need. Such information, when traded off or spilled, can spell the end for an organization or association. Information, for example, monetary records and other strategic data, client login accreditations, require capacity where recuperation is helpful and simple. Store information as per need is dependent on the significance of the information to the business.

(6). Reinforcement of Important Data – Every organization has some basic information, which is indispensable. Henceforth, every recuperation or reinforcement plan ought to incorporate making duplicates of anything that is not replaceable. In a Managed Service Provider's (MSP) case, it incorporates documents, information on client and worker records, business messages, and so on [7]. The arrangement set up ought to encourage snappy recuperation so organizations can recuperate tomorrow from any catastrophe that happens today.

(7). Ensure Hard Copy Data – Electronic or computerized information is the fundamental focal point of the present-day IT security systems [8]. There is as yet a huge volume of actual archives that organizations need to look after every day.

For instance, an ordinary MSP includes working with a grouping of duty records, agreements, and representative documents, which are pretty much as significant as the information saved money on the hard drives. Convert archives that can be digitized to limit the deficiency of actual reports.

(8). Design a Recovery Plan – Disasters can possibly clear out an organization's server farm totally.

Organizations ought to plan for the most noticeably terrible, by assigning an optional site that would go about as a backup for the essential site. The subsequent site ought to be furnished with the necessary devices and frameworks to recuperate influenced frameworks to guarantee that the business measures proceed.

(9). Establishing a Communication Program – Communication inside the organization is indispensable in the midst of an emergency. Organizations ought to consider drafting test messages ahead of time to assist in correspondence with providers and accomplices amid an emergency.

Business Continuity groups can utilize a definite correspondence intended to organize their endeavours effectively.

(10). Testing and Updation – Every significant business program ought to be tried and estimated for its viability, and business progression plans are no special cases [9]. Testing ought to incorporate running re-enactments to test the group's degree of readiness during an emergency. In light of the outcomes, extra alterations and changes can be made.

3. ROLE OF CYBER SECURITY IN BUSINESS RESILIENCE

As we know the major aim behind cybersecurity is to prevent all attacks with a 100 percent guarantee which is not at all possible with any technique. In general, an attacker simply aims at finding only one vulnerable point. Due to this fact, it is almost impossible to prevent these cyber-attacks with 100 percent accuracy.

Cybersecurity's role extends beyond merely detecting or blocking cyber threats; a significant part of its mandate is to institute cyber resilience. This ensures that operations and productivity remain unaffected in the event of a cyber-attack. To foster cyber resilience, it is imperative to comprehend the business context of a compromise: understanding which business services are or could be impacted, and deciphering the implications for the business.

3.1. Reducing Cyber Risk

Visualizing the attack surface in relation to business services enables organizations to prioritize their mitigation efforts. Today's digital landscape is a complex mix of hybrid and multi-cloud environments, coupled with container technologies to manage independent applications and a plethora of Internet-of-Things (IoT) technologies. Some of these are categorized as SaaS applications [10].

A cyber asset attack surface management (CAASM) solution provides visibility of internal assets. This enables us to identify gaps in security controls and reveal weaknesses in the security posture that need to be addressed and remediated. Therefore, to build cyber resiliency, one has to start with a comprehensive and unifying mapping of the entire enterprise's digital estate. One of the approaches is to take periodic snapshots which are apparently not inadequate because IT environments are constantly shifting and evolving. In order to make it effective, we have to have real-time, continuous management and inventory controls of all assets, apps, and users to effectively improve threat response and security controls. The following step-by-step approach can be applied in that case:

- Discover and visualize every application, every identity, and every relationship (and data flows) across the enterprise environment to map the total attack surface.
- Observe the interactions across all of these identities to establish a baseline for normal activity so you can recognize anomalous actions or behaviour.
- Establish and verify consistent application-centric access control policies to natively enforce security across your existing infrastructure and applications.

As we have already witnessed that understanding the business context of applications and their relationships completely is not at all possible so that one can reduce the attack surface. Still, it can reduce the chances of a successful cyberattack and improve cyber resilience for the organization.

CONCLUSION AND FUTURE WORK

The relationship between business resilience and data breaches is complex, involving numerous dynamic components. Establishing robust and adaptable frameworks is crucial to ensuring the ability to pivot when necessary, maintaining business momentum regardless of the encountered circumstances. We hope that readers take away one key message from this article: your response to a crisis will significantly influence the severity of a data breach's impact on your organization and the duration of your recovery period.

REFERENCES

[1]   Available from: https://www.csis.org/news/cybersecurity-agenda-45th-president

[2]   Available from: http://www.rand.org/content/dam/rand/pubs/research_reports/RR400/RR430/RAND_RR430.pdf

[3]   Available from: http://www.ccc.edu/news/Pages/Applications-Now-Available-for-City-Colleges-of-Chicagos-New-Cyber-Security-Boot-Camp-.aspx

[4]   Available   from: http://www.giac.org/paper/gsec/1641/implementing-network-security-metrics-programs/103004

[5]   Yan. Huang, and P. Yang, "Research of security metric architecture for next generation network", *Proceedings of IC: NIDC,* 2009.

[6]   K. Scarfone, and P. Mell, *The Common configuration scoring system (CCSS): Metrics for software security configuration vulnerabilities (Draft).* National Institute of Standards and Technology. Available on: Gaithersburg, MD, 2009. Available from: https://csrc.nist.gov/publications/drafts/nistir-7502/Draft-NISTIR-7502.pdf

[7]   C. Justin, B. Ivan, K. Arvind, and A. Tom, "Seattle: A platform for educational cloud computing", *SIGCSE09, March 37, 2009,* Chattanooga, Tennessee, USA. 2009.

[8]   M. Armbrust, A. Fox, R. Griffith, A. Joseph, R. Katz, A. Konwinski, G. Lee, D. Patterson, A. Rabkin, I. Stoica, and M. Zaharia, "Above the clouds: A berkeley view of cloud computing", *UCBerkeley Reliable Adaptive Distributed Systems Laboratory,* 2009.

[9]   Available from: https://www.techtarget.com/iotagenda/definition/Internet-of-Things-IoT

[10]   F. Bonomi, R. Milito, J. Zhu, and S. Addepalli, "Fog computing and its role in the internet of things", In: *Proceedings of the First Edition of the MCC Workshop on Mobile Cloud Computing, ser. MCC '12* ACM: New York, NY, USA, 2012, pp. 13-16.
       [http://dx.doi.org/10.1145/2342509.2342513]

CHAPTER 8

Security and Privacy of Application of Smart Cities

Amit Garg[1,*], **Ashish Kumar**[2] and **Ankur Rastogi**[3]

[1] *IIMT Engineering College, Meerut, Uttar Pradesh, India*

[2] *ITS Engineering College, Greater Noida, Uttar Pradesh, India*

[3] *Jain University, Bengaluru, Karnataka, India*

Abstract: In this chapter, we have discussed smart cities, their applications, and the associated security and privacy issues. We will begin with a brief introduction to smart cities, followed by a focus on the major and essential applications required to transform a city into a smart city. We will cover topics such as smart education, healthcare, governance, transportation, and services. Each of these applications plays a crucial and efficient role in realizing the objectives of a smart city. Furthermore, it is imperative to address the security and privacy concerns related to these applications, particularly concerning data access and protection, and to identify the necessary security requirements for these applications.

Keywords: Smart city, Security, Smart city applications.

1. INTRODUCTION

The size and population of urban areas are steadily increasing, as indicated by global estimate reports. Consequently, the day-to-day challenges in metropolitan areas are intensifying due to limited resources and services such as healthcare, education, environment, and transportation. To maintain the sustainability of these services in urban areas, innovative strategies for effective data management must be prioritized. The term 'smart city' derives from the integration of mobile computing systems through practical data management networks across all components and layers of the city itself. Cities are increasingly focusing their efforts on becoming smarter through the use of data management networks, such as the Internet of Things (IoT), big data, and cloud computing technologies [1]. These comprehensive systems enhance various aspects of operations and services, including traffic management, sustainable resource management, quality of life, and infrastructure in the smart city.

---

* **Corresponding author Amit Garg:** IIMT Engineering College, Meerut, Uttar Pradesh, India; E-mail: foramitgarg@gmail.com

Samayveer Singh , Manju, Aruna Malik, and Pradeep Kumar Singh (Eds.)

The rapid advancement of IoT technologies motivates researchers and scientists to create new application areas and services, and these novel smart services must adequately address the needs of citizens worldwide. Furthermore, to promote awareness of smart city concepts globally, human needs must be considered through the exchange and collection of data within IoT services. Therefore, the network should be embedded with sensing, computing, networking, and actuation capabilities. Another major goal is to monitor, collect, archive, and share public sensor data from IoT devices to facilitate the development and analysis of smart cities.

In the current literature, a vast array of studies addresses various key topics related to smart cities. Examples include environmental monitoring for smart urban areas, quality of life for residents in a smart city (with a specific focus on four city-scale phenomena: weather, public transportation, and people flows), as well as data aggregation and quality analysis in a semantic web environment within smart cities. Various applications of smart cities are illustrated in Fig. (1). The existing literature contributes to research on different components such as smart people, smart economy, smart governance, smart mobility, smart environment, and smart living. However, the definitions of these terms vary across numerous articles, and these components change according to preferences. For instance, one smart city might focus on a disaster management system, falling under the category of the smart community theme, while another city might prioritize integrating the waste management system into the urban infrastructure [2].

These days, more than 54 percent of the world's population resides in urban areas, and by 2050, this percentage is expected to reach 66 percent. The rapid population growth, coupled with increased urbanization, has given rise to a variety of technical, social, economic, and administrative challenges that tend to threaten the efficient and environmental sustainability of cities. As a result, many governments have been showing interest in adopting "smart" concepts to enhance the utilization and management of both tangible and intangible assets. The 'smart city' concept refers to the application of all available technology and resources in an intelligent and coordinated manner, aiming to develop urban centers that are at once integrated, livable, and sustainable [3]. The smart city boasts a range of remarkable applications in contemporary societies. Examples include smart energy, which enhances the generation, monitoring, and consumption of various types of energy and resources using digital technologies; smart buildings, which autonomously control and manage lighting and temperature systems, security, and energy consumption throughout large constructions; smart mobility, which enables intelligent transportation through innovative and integrated technologies and solutions; smart technology, which facilitates intelligent network connectivity and edge processing solutions in cities worldwide; smart healthcare, which enables intelligent systems and connected medical devices to promote health, provide health monitoring, and diagnostics; and smart governance and education, which offer digital services and policies from the government and foster the educational system through cutting-edge technologies. Additionally, there is smart security, aimed at reducing security risks and providing managed security services to protect people, properties, and information.

2. SMART CITIES APPLICATIONS

Building a smart city aims to benefit inhabitants in various aspects closely related to the standard of living of residents, such as energy, environment, industry, living, and governance, as illustrated in Fig (**1**).

2.1. Smart Government

The smart government plays a pivotal role in a smart city. Its purpose is to better serve citizens and communities by interconnecting data, networks, processes, and physical infrastructures based on information technology. Additionally, smart governance enables citizens to participate in public decisions and city planning, enhancing efficiency while increasing information transparency. For example, e-government allows individuals to access governmental services online, such as scheduling appointments, paying bills, and reporting issues [4].

2.2. Smart Transportation

Smart transportation aims to provide a 'smarter' use of transport systems. Specifically, smart transportation networks can better serve the public by enhancing safety, speed, and reliability. Using transport-oriented mobile applications, consumers can easily organize their schedules and find the most economical and fastest routes. Other common applications in smart transportation include driver's licenses, license recognition systems, and vehicle parking, among others.

2.3. Smart Environment

A smart environment can contribute significantly to building a sustainable society. Specifically, by adopting technical management tools, a smart city can monitor energy consumption, air quality, structural stability of buildings, and traffic congestion, efficiently addressing pollution or waste. Ideally, novel environmental sensor networks might even be capable of predicting and identifying natural disasters in the future.

2.4. Smart Utilities

Smart utilities enable the smart city to reduce the overconsumption of resources such as water and gas, improving economic growth and contributing to environmental protection. Smart metering, a practical smart utility application, is commonly applied in smart grids to monitor distributed energy resources. Additionally, smart water meters and smart light sensors are used to manage resources and reduce energy loss.

2.5. Smart Services

Smart services benefit citizens in many aspects. For example, smart healthcare applications can timely monitor individuals' health conditions through wearable devices and medical sensors. Furthermore, some smart services can create comfortable, intelligent, and energy-saving living conditions, such as through the remote control of home appliances. Last but not least, social networking, entertainment, smart shopping, and other smart services have considerably improved the convenience of people's daily lives [5].

2.6. Smart Energy

Smart energy, as a vital application of the smart city, is responsible for providing a livable, affordable, environmentally friendly, and engaging environment for the citizens. The objective of smart energy is to efficiently manage energy and resource consumption and increase the utilization of renewable energy sources based on an integrated and adaptable resource system, as well as intelligence-driven and pioneering approaches to strategic planning.

2.7. Smart Building

Smart building refers to a dynamic way of measuring, monitoring, controlling, and optimizing operations and maintenance by exploiting progressive automation and integration. ICT plays a significant role in the development and operation of smart buildings, generating real-time responses to the continuously increasing flow of data based on analytics and data management. In summary, the data produced by the sensors, monitors, and controllers of the smart building can be collected and analyzed in real time to monitor everything. One of the main uses of smart buildings is to manage the energy equipment by automatically responding to both internal settings and external signals, reducing energy consumption, and increasing energy reliability [6].

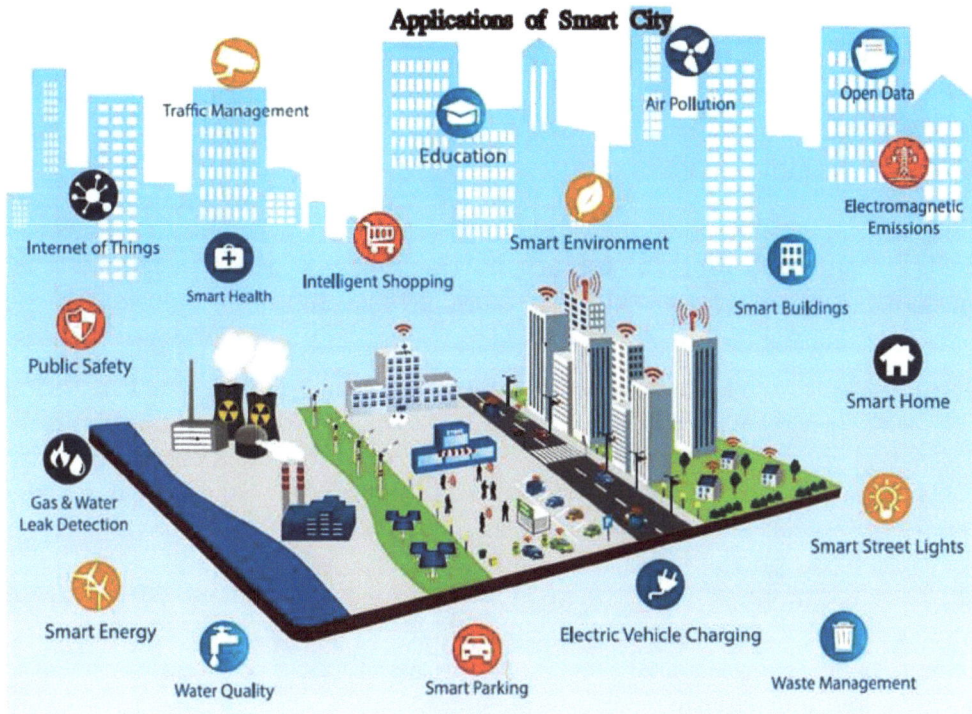

Fig. (1). Smart city.

2.8. Smart Mobility

Smart mobility offers a compelling method for moving people and goods, aiming to achieve a seamless and sustainable society through the optimization of various transportation services for residents. This is achieved by integrating diverse transportation modes within cities. One way to establish a smart mobility system for a city is to build a network for collecting, processing, and analyzing data from the existing transportation systems of various organizations.

2.9. Smart Education

Smart education significantly improves the operational performance of cities and nurtures new generations for life in the complex world of the future. The advantages of smart education can be observed from different perspectives. On one hand, from the infrastructure perspective, implementing an intelligent system can help educational centers maintain comprehensive control and management over their energy systems, security levels, communication, and transportation. On the other hand, the intelligent system of smart education can provide new facilities for students by incorporating current technologies or social media, such as virtual, online, and e-learning [7].

2.10. Smart Health-Care

Shows offering wellbeing administrations based on setting mindful organization, and ICT framework of brilliant urban communities. Smart Healthcare is a progressive idea, which normally has consequences for some detects:

i. Society: Enhancing healthcare services can undeniably contribute to creating a healthier society where citizens focus more on proper nutrition and physical activity, and patients can benefit from effective treatments at minimal cost.
ii. Government: Implementing smart healthcare can significantly reduce healthcare costs for the government, for example, by strengthening the detection and prevention mechanisms.
iii. Research: Adopting a smart healthcare model in society results in the collection of a vast amount of data, which researchers can use to perform experiments to gain insights into various aspects of human behavior, healthcare, and patterns [8, 9].

3. SECURITY AND PRIVACY ISSUES IN APPLICATIONS OF SMART CITIES

Recently, significant issues have surfaced in various application scenarios within smart cities. For instance, the smart metering system in smart grids can monitor the private lives of residents, revealing their living habits and working hours. Additionally, in the realms of smart homes and healthcare, device manufacturers and service providers may gain access to sensitive data. Furthermore, the extensive amount of direction information collected by intelligent mobility applications can be utilized to infer a user's location and mobility patterns. Beyond these issues, there are other pressing concerns arising from the rapidly developing smart applications [10].

3.1. Botnet Activities in IoT-Based Applications

As of late arose IoT botnets have presented genuine dangers to IoT frameworks. An agent model is the Mirai botnet, which can contaminate gadgets, spread disease to numerous heterogeneous IoT gadgets, and lastly cause a DDoS against target workers. Contrasted and PCs and advanced cells, IoT gadgets are regularly planned with helpless security or even none by any stretch of the imagination. Tragically, this threat was not understood until the second 50% of 2016. Hence, considerably more work is required, and the security local area ought to create novel protections. Something else, this new type of DDoS assault will destructively affect the IoT-empowered biological system.

3.2. Threats of Driverless Cars in Smart Cities

Cutting-edge organisations have spent billions of dollars creating self-governing vehicles (AVs), planning to decrease auto collisions, and constructing a cleaner and more smart society. Nonetheless, this quickly developing application has been viewed as a significant security issue because once an AV is hacked, both life well-being and information protection will be compromised. In particular, programmers can misuse security bugs to direct distant assaults, for example, by applying the brakes, closing down the motor, and controlling the guiding. Furthermore, the huge individual information gathered by the PC arrangement of a self-driving vehicle may cause critical security issues [11].

3.3. Privacy Issues of Virtual Reality in Applications

In innovation-driven smart urban communities, augmented reality (VR) innovation has been grasped by different associations and elements, for example, city arranging offices, medical care specialist organizations, and the designing business area. Be that as it may, the delicate data imparted to outsiders, the decoded interchanges between VR gadgets, and the information put away by sensors all posture dangers of protection spillage. Sadly, because these new applications are raced to market, planners and clients have not made proper and thorough protection contemplations.

3.4. Threats Posed by AI in Applications

Simulated intelligence frameworks assume fundamental parts in different smart applications, for example, programmed control of exchanging frameworks, home machines, and pacemakers. Notwithstanding, the developing utilization of AI likewise presents security chances. For instance, specialist co-ops and gadget makers can utilize information mining advances to exorbitantly investigate individual information and extricate delicate data that surpass the essential destinations of the connected administrations. Moreover, assailants with information on AI are additionally getting more intelligent. Programmers may see how ML-based assurance instruments were prepared or planned with the goal that they can embrace focused on ways to deal with debilitated preparation impacts and to diminish the dependability of the calculations.

4. SECURITY REQUIREMENTS OF APPLICATIONS

While smart cities facilitate our lives and assist us in managing and controlling various aspects of our environment, the increased complexity, interdependencies, and connectivity render smart cities more vulnerable to security and privacy attacks. A limited understanding or lack of awareness of the security challenges and requirements of a smart city may lead to unacceptable and insecure implementations and operations of the smart city. In this section, we will discuss the key requirements for a secure smart city, which must be taken into account during the planning stage. These security requirements have been identified through extensive studies of smart cities, utilizing various keywords such as security, requirement, smart city, IoT, big data, cloud, cloud of things, fog, and edge [12].

4.1. Secure Communication

Organizational correspondence is known as a fundamental segment of the smart city models to join various parts of the smart city for gathering, sharing, and moving information all through the urban communities. Setting up a safe wire and remote correspondence in smart urban areas relies upon classification, uprightness, and non-disavowal as the significant highlights of organization security. Perhaps the most ideal approach to make sure about the smart urban areas interchanges is to create lightweight cryptographic strategies for scrambling and decoding information and making a divided mystery key between different hubs. Notwithstanding, applying such security calculations to various organisation parts is a vital test in smart urban areas because of the heterogeneity of the gadgets that are associated with the organisation and used to gather or share information. The following test for making the correspondence secure is to plan a powerful dispersed key administration framework for giving secure communication because of the geological appropriation of smart urban communities. The key administration community ordinarily creates the essential keys (public and private keys) with legitimate length and lifetime for all parts to meet the security targets and simultaneously not channel the inserted framework's assets.

4.2. Secure Booting

Worms, viruses, and other malware can overpower the frameworks through the boot areas wherein such security issues are situated as an executable code and can be conveyed to different frameworks through the Internet association or after booting the other framework utilising tainted circles. Pre-boot malware is additionally ready to be executed before the framework is constrained by utilising an Operating System (OS) portion and afterwards hung out in manners that are unthinkable for the OS and Issue scanners to identify the malware. Without a doubt, a secure boot is planned as an extra layer to ensure the framework against the pre-boot measure. Secure booting is an innovation for causing the framework firmware to check the presence of a cryptographic mark for the framework boot loader. Since the cryptographic key of the mark is put away in the firmware data set, it is hard for the malware maker to sign the malware if the key is constrained by the approved client. Subsequently, the firmware will not execute the program, which contains the unsigned malware. The firmware can likewise check malware based on a cryptographically produced computerised signature in the following stage: boot loader, bit, and client space. All in all, the safe boot is a required innovation for smart city gadgets that ensures the uprightness and the legitimacy of the product bundles and dodges the execution of unsigned code.

4.3. Security Monitoring, Analysis, and Response

Checking methodology is a fundamental essential for all frameworks to control the general climate and distinguish the dynamic assaults and unknown conduct. The mechanised reaction frameworks should approach satisfactory data about assaults and programmed discovery of dubious conduct because of the adaptability of IoT frameworks as far as the number of gadgets and the measure of data being prepared. The framework may think about various techniques for reacting to assaults and dicey conduct: (i) Elimination methodology to briefly disconnect, isolate, or totally eliminate such pieces of IoT gadgets, and (ii) Response procedure in which a proper occurrence reaction measure is considered to adapt to weaknesses that are recognised upon the frameworks have been placed into administration.

4.4. System, Application, and Solution Lifecycle Management

As it is clear, smart urban areas depend on IoT gadgets to gather, examine, and connect with the residents. Accordingly, expanding the interest in IoT arrangements brings about building up the application without bargaining security and decreasing the execution of the framework. In any case, the venture clients anticipate that the designers should envision the need for frameworks sooner rather than later. Besides, the important activities and plans for the whole life pattern of IoT gadgets and applications must be anticipated at various plan phases of brilliant urban communities. The lifecycle of the executives of the IoT frameworks needs a significant level of unpredictability and has an immediate connection with the character of the board, a gadget, and advancement of use and programming by altering the administration of sent and in-administration frameworks. The need to interface any kind of gadget, even those that are not intended for availability, powers the IoT framework designers to ensure the security of such associations. Subsequently, engineers need to think about defensive measures at all levels of devices, organisations, and the cloud. Additionally, the designers need to approve the code, key material, and even actual segments of such frameworks in all phases of advancement and establishment. After safely associating, the IoT gadgets should have the ability to safely overhaul their unmistakable segments to beat the weaknesses, accomplish utilitarian upgrades over the lifetime of the framework, and ensure the protection and security of information. At long last, it needs to address the test of coordinating the IoT gadgets with other city frameworks that can total, investigate, and act after gathering the information from gadgets, to make an extension between operational innovation and data innovation frameworks [13].

4.5. Updating and Patching

Refreshing and fixing are the significant necessities of IoT gadgets to work appropriately and be secure against the latest pernicious assaults. This is because by building up the innovation, we are confronting the new and complex security assaults that may not be defeated except if getting the product refreshes. Besides, it permits the endeavours to distinguish the weaknesses and address them proficiently. The gadgets ought to likewise have an inclination for verifying the patches through their administrators and specialist co-ops. Be that as it may, the confirmation cycle should not have any result on the utilitarian well-being of an IoT gadget and its interconnection with different gadgets, particularly when they are responsible for performing imperative tasks and need security patches to be ensured against weaknesses. Mention that the product refreshes and the security patches ought to be given in a compacted bundle to be downloadable through the restricted data transfer capacity and decrease the likelihood of bargaining practical wellbeing.

4.6. Authentication, Identification, and Access Control

The force of IoT frameworks and gadgets is profoundly subject to sharing information and consolidating various contributions just as preparing and making extra qualities. Therefore, it is crucial to control and deal with the produced information by other IoT gadgets while forestalling the utilisation of information in unapproved or undesired ways. The validation of IoT frameworks by building secure correspondence between the included things is a critical pre-requisite for smart urban communities to deal with the entrance control of the legitimated residents in an approved way and forestall unapproved clients from getting to assets. To build a strong correspondence, diverse validation, and access control conventions, for example, Identity-Based Encryption (IBE), Attribute-Based Encryption (ABE), and Role-Based Access Control (RBAC), have been intended to ensure the security and protection of information, particularly in cloud-based smart urban communities. This is because the residents' data is gathered and moved to the conveyed information stockpiles, which are controlled and overseen by unapproved Cloud Service providers (CSPs). These plans empower shrewd city applications to safely deal with the approved clients and repudiate their consent rights. For instance, the goal of characteristic-based admittance control is to deliver the current credits of the information proprietor, clients, or other IoT gadgets to execute the information access control.

CONCLUSION

We have described and classified a wide range of exploration zones related to smart city applications, with the aim of focusing on security and privacy issues and ways to address them. We began by elucidating the smart city concept based on digital cities and ICT cities, examining their features. Moreover, we have presented comprehensive information on the security and privacy of smart cities and their applications, focusing on security requirements, issues, and challenges. The widespread use of intelligent applications has led to numerous security and privacy issues. The development of more advanced protection models and mechanisms is crucial and in high demand in both industrial and academic fields. Inspired by these factors, we describe the latest efforts and advancements in countermeasures from the perspectives of various disciplines. We also explored current issues and open challenges that have emerged recently, laying the groundwork for further studies. Various protection mechanisms and strategies have been developed recently. However, there is still a long way to go to meet the numerous security requirements of these rapidly developing smart applications. It is reasonable to expect that in the coming years, mitigating the presented challenges will be the primary task of smart city-related studies. Finally, various open issues have been identified as significant challenges for future research directions.

REFERENCES

[1]   A. Kirimtat, O. Krejcar, A. Kertesz, and M.F. Tasgetiren, "Future trends and current state of smart city concepts: A survey", *IEEE Access,* vol. 8, pp. 86448-86467, 2020.
[http://dx.doi.org/10.1109/ACCESS.2020.2992441]

[2]   F. Sivrikaya, N. Ben-Sassi, X.T. Dang, O.C. Görür, and C. Kuster, "Internet of smart city objects: A distributed framework for service discovery and composition", *IEEE Access,* vol. 7, pp. 14434-14454,

2019.
[http://dx.doi.org/10.1109/ACCESS.2019.2893340]

[3]   S. Al-Nasrawi, A. El-Zaart, and C. Adams, "Assessing smartness of smart, sustainable cities: A comparative analysis", In: *2017 Sensors Networks Smart and Emerging Technologies* SENSET: Beirut, 2017, pp. 1-4.

[4]   L. Cui, G. Xie, Y. Qu, L. Gao, and Y. Yang, "Security and privacy in smart cities: Challenges and opportunities", *IEEE Access,* vol. 6, pp. 46134-46145, 2018.
[http://dx.doi.org/10.1109/ACCESS.2018.2853985]

[5]   H. Attaran, N. Kheibari, and D. Bahrepour, "Toward integrated smart city: A new model for implementation and design challenges", *GeoJ.,* vol. 87, no. S4, suppl. 4, pp. 511-526, 2022.
[http://dx.doi.org/10.1007/s10708-021-10560-w] [PMID: 35075319]

[6]   H. Samih, "Smart cities and internet of things", *J. Inform. Technol. Case and Applic. Res.,* vol. 21, no. 1, 2019.

[7]   B. Hamid, N. Jhanjhi, M. Humayun, A. Khan, and A. Alsayat, "Cyber security issues and challenges for smart cities: A survey", *PRISED tangle: A privacy-aware framework for smart healthcare data sharing using IOTA tangle,* Complex & Intelligent Systems 10, 2022.
[http://dx.doi.org/10.1109/MACS48846.2019.9024768]

[8]   E. Bandauko, and R.N. Arku, "A critical analysis of 'smart cities' as an urban development strategy in Africa", *Int. Plann. Stud.,* vol. 0, no. 0, pp. 1-18, 2022.

[9]   Sidrah Abdullah, Junaid Arshad, Muhammad Mubashir Khan, Mamoun Alazab, and Khaled Salah, "PRISED tangle: A privacy-aware framework for smart healthcare data sharing using IOTA tangle", *Complex & Intelligent Systems 10,* 2022.

[10]   S. Tousley, and S. Rhee, "Smart and secure cities and communities", In: *IEEE International Science of Smart City Operations and Platforms Engineering in Partnership with Global City Teams Challenge.* SCOPE-GCTC: Porto, 2018.

[11]   M. Houichi, F. Jaidi, and A. Bouhoula, "Analysis of smart cities security: Challenges and advancements", *15th International Conference on Security of Information and Networks (SIN),* pages 01-05, 2022.
[http://dx.doi.org/10.1109/SIN56466.2022.9970494]

[12]   M.A. Merline, and R. Vimalathithan, "Smart city: Issues and research challenges in implementation", *IEEE International Conference on Smart Grid and Smart Cities (ICSGSC),* pp. 263-266, 2017.
[http://dx.doi.org/10.1109/ICSGSC.2017.8038588]

[13]   N. Alsaffar, H. Ali, and W. Elmedany, "Smart transportation system: A review of security and privacy issues", *2018 International Conference on Innovation and Intelligence for Informatics, Computing, and Technologies (3ICT),* Sakhier, Bahrain, 2018, pp. 1-4.
[http://dx.doi.org/10.1109/3ICT.2018.8855737]

CHAPTER 9

Security Metric for Information Network

Saurabh Singhal[1,*] and **Manju**[2]

[1] *Department of Computer Science and Engineering, Apex Institute of Technology, Chandigarh University, Chandigarh, India*

[2] *Department of Computer Science and Information Technology, Jaypee Institute of Information Technology, Noida, Uttar Pradesh, India*

Abstract: Given that dislodged working conditions are in play, system administrators are tasked with handling security solutions that, in turn, impact most of the working layers of the OSI model. This comprehensive approach depicts a situation in which the originator perceives that their data is traversing through a specified encryption process at every stage/layer, starting from the top layer (*i.e.*, Application Layer) and gradually proceeding down to the last one (*i.e.*, Physical Layer). Similarly, the decryption process takes place at every stage/layer at the destination end.

Keywords: Network security, OSI model, Security metrics.

1. INTRODUCTION

In the Internet of Things (IoT) era, the widespread propagation of networks has made network access easier, subsequently allowing a more comprehensive range of unauthorised users to exploit vulnerabilities. Powerful encryption algorithms like the Advanced Encryption Standard (AES) and the Protection in Depth approach are employed to address emerging threats [1]. This work aims to highlight several shortcomings embedded in various layers of the Open Systems Interconnection particularly focusing on issues related to the 8th layer. Growing lapses in cybersecurity within the military sector have led to an increased risk of embedded malware and cyber-attacks from harmful entities and nations, highlighting the growing importance of the new domain of cryptography. At the same time, the accessibility of IoT device networks by a more extensive base has increased the chances of unauthorised access by hackers aiming to exploit these systems. This risk can be mitigated by deploying more complex security algorithms [2].

---

[*] **Corresponding author Saurabh Singhal:** Department of Computer Science and Engineering, Apex Institute of Technology, Chandigarh University, Chandigarh, India; E-mail: saurabh.singhal09@gmail.com

Samayveer Singh , Manju, Aruna Malik, and Pradeep Kumar Singh (Eds.)

2. RELATED WORKS

Network security consists of the policies, procedures, programs, hardware, software, and people you use to protect your corporate IoT network. In general, network security aims to stop unauthorised access to sensitive information, which mainly includes protected health information (PHI) data, payment card industry (PCI) data, and sometimes corporate financials or intellectual properties [3].

The following are the fundamental terms related to network security [4, 5]:

- **Authentication** – This is related to multi-factor authentication, where a user's ID and password are needed to access any application or data stored by some organisation. Most critical industries do not use single-factor authentication (like passwords), as it is pretty easy to retrieve or crack passwords.
- **Firewalls** – It controls the incoming and outgoing overthe network. Nowadays, organizations need to configure firewalls according to their requirement, which is imposed by the application usage.
- **Antivirus, Intrusion Detection, and Intrusion Management Systems** – Firewalls may not be able to catch everything, especially viruses and worms, so antivirus, intrusion detection (IDS), and Security Information and Event Management (SIEM) systems can help detect and stop malware.
- **Encryption** – To enhance security at theorganizational level, they sometimes use various encryption techniques to communicate within the network. This way, they can further protect the data from outsiders.

Apart from these four areas, which are basically followed by small organizations, large corporate networks, and structures enforce a variety of ways to secure their critical data. Below are some more techniques followed by these large organizations to increase network security:

- **Penetration testing** (also known as "ethical hacking") – Penetration testing is a service that involves a professional penetration tester uncovering network security weaknesses.
- **Vulnerability scanning** identifies big risks such as misconfigured firewalls, malware hazards, and remote access vulnerabilities.
- **On-site audits** – Depending on whether you are working towards security mandate compliance (PCI, GDPR, HIPAA), you may need to schedule an onsite audit for your organization.
- **Remediation** –There are some IT teams that can open and close ports on your network and also check someone's activity and regularly install patches.

2.1. Gray Area Network

Due to large businesses and organizations operating with one central headquarters and numerous smaller remote or satellite locations—including telecommuting employees—security efforts, while often focused on the headquarters, must also consider these remote areas as critical to overall network security.

In some cases, organizations have seen their entire headquarters' operations held ransom by malware initially downloaded onto the network through a remote franchise location. Such situations arise due to a portion of the network known as the 'gray area,' which tends to surround remote locations, creating ambiguity around responsibility for security. Questions arise: Is it the headquarters that is responsible for data security and compliance, the franchise, or the telecommuting employees? How reliable is their home network's security [6, 7]. In these scenarios, the main question becomes: Who is responsible? The employee or the corporation? The company does not own the employee's network, yet that network presents a very real vulnerability. Risks increase significantly when there is little to no visibility into these gray area networks. This lack of visibility is also why remote network owners often hesitate to provide insight into their networks, typically citing privacy concerns. However, when remote connections are allowed into your network, you automatically assume some responsibility for any threats that the network may pose, whether you wish to or not.

Therefore, the major concern that arises is: what can be done to help mitigate the risks that gray area networks present to your network while ensuring privacy and control are maintained by the respective network owners [8, 9].

For a large organisation or franchise with numerous remote locations, it becomes crucial to find a network security company capable of providing a level of visibility into your gray area networks to monitor for threats.

To address these issues, the International Standard Organization (ISO) has introduced a layered approach to communication, aiming to overcome the challenges posed by unstructured communication, where the aforementioned threats are more inevitable. ISO's theoretical model provides characterization and standardization of a communication system, dividing it into layers. Created by the International Standard Organization (ISO), this model unifies similar communicating functions into a single layer. Each layer provides services to the one above it and receives services from the layer below [10, 11]. The application and implementation domains of the OSI model are so diverse that it defines how industries related to Information Technology should frame and postulate their networking protocols and rules. The development of each layer is done independently, making them flexible, and enhancements in one layer can be made without affecting the others [12]. The process of encapsulation is followed as information passes through each layer, with specific information concerning a specific layer attached.

3. SYSTEM MODEL

We are discussing vulnerabilities at every layer:

(A). Physical Layer – This layer consists of issues such as the disconnection of physical data links, dissemination of power, control of the environmental conditions, keystroke and other input logging, physical damage to data and hardware, theft of data and hardware, and unwanted changes to the functional environment, such as adding or removing resources, data connections, and media. There is also the challenge of undetectable interception of data. These issues are more prominent in the case of a wireless network, where a subsequent transmission over the network can easily influence the quality of service. The likelihood of passive, inactive, or indirect attacks on such a network is very high.

(B). Data Link Layer – A device operating in promiscuous mode alongside a packet filter can be either a supportive or adversarial tool at OSI Layer 2. Allowing for flow analysis, trouble resolution, and code debugging can be beneficial. However, the ability to replicate datagrams can pose a threat when in the wrong hands. An example of a Layer 2 threat is Libpcap, a packet capture driver that forces an NIC (Network Interface Card) into promiscuous mode, allowing it to capture traffic destined for other machines. Known threats at Layer 2 include Address Resolution Protocol (ARP) attacks, Content-Addressable Memory (CAM) table overflow, Private VLAN attacks, DHCP Starvation, Spanning Tree Protocol Manipulation, VLAN hopping, Media Access Control (MAC) Address Spoofing, and more.

(C). Network Layer – At this layer, one can adopt either a procedural approach or a combination of both to transfer variable length data sequences from a source in one network to a host in a different network, in contrast to the data link layer which connects sender and receiver hosts within the same or a similar network. This layer also ensures the quality of service requested by the transport layer is maintained. The IP address enables a device to communicate with the outside world and allows the outside world to reach the host. It is a critical boundary to consider when assessing device vulnerability. Key security concerns for the Network Layer related to IP include ICMP (Internet Control Message Protocol) attacks, IP Spoofing, Ping of Death Attacks, Routing (RIP) Attacks, Teardrop Attacks, ICMP Flood, and Packet Sniffing.

(D). Transport Layer – The main responsibility of the Transport Layer is to ensure reliable, error-checked communication, primarily managed through TCP

(Transmission Control Protocol) Connection-Oriented Communication. Another protocol used at Layer 4 is UDP (User Datagram Protocol) Connectionless Communication. To locate a device on the Internet, you need to know its public IP address. To target a specific application on a specific device, an attacker would need to know both the IP address to locate the device and the port number assigned to the application, together known as a socket. Generally, all 65535 ports on any device can be further divided into three main categories: Dynamic, Registered, and Well-Known. This is where Layer 4 security is implemented and applied. Many applications use well-known TCP and UDP ports, making it easier for attackers to gather information about a system by scanning these ports.

(E). Session Layer – The 'session' is established using a three-way handshaking mechanism for data communication. When a client attempts to connect to a specific server, the client must send a well-defined SYN request; after receiving this request, the server responds with an SYN/ACK packet, and then upon receiving this acknowledgment, the client further validates it. Typically, the TCP connection waits until all these steps are completed.

(F). Presentation Layer –The primary function of this layer is to encode and encrypt data for transmission across a network, sometimes referred to as the Syntax Layer. The more sophisticated and complex the encryption algorithm, the more challenging it is to access the data. This intensive processing requirement can impact device performance. Appropriate planning is crucial to balance security needs and maintain system performance. Exploiting the environment of implied trust and simplicity that systems were (and continue to be) built upon, attackers have fed unexpected or illegal input to presentation layer services, achieving results that are undesirable or far from what the original designers intended [16]. Some tactics employed include attacking the NetBIOS, buffer overflows, and format string vulnerabilities.

(G). Application Layer – The Application Layer is closest to the end-user or destination system, meaning that the OSI application layer and the user interact directly with the software application. Functions of the application layer typically involve identifying resource availability, establishing communication partners, and synchronizing communication [17]. When establishing communication partners, the application layer determines the identity and availability of communication partners for an application with data to transmit to a specific destination. Like the physical layer, the open-ended nature of the Application Layer amalgamates various threats at its end of the stack. Some of these include access attacks, authentication attacks, backdoor attacks, and phishing attacks.

(H). The Eight Layer – Human Layer – A common misconception about the Open Systems Interconnection model is that it comprises only seven layers. However, there exists an eighth layer above 'Application,' commonly referred to as the 'User' or 'Human Layer.' This is also known as Neuman's Layer. This eighth layer must be acknowledged and considered during network troubleshooting, as it is frequently a more prevalent cause of issues than the physical layer. A mistake, or a deliberate act of tampering with any of the above layers by this eighth layer entity, can cause devastation throughout the network. Common causes of failures at the Eighth layer of the OSI model include ID10T errors and policy-related issues. Considering how the eighth layer communicates directly with the application layer, a problem at the eighth layer can cause issues at other layers, with varying degrees of severity depending on network security and privilege settings. Layer eight issues can even lead to failures at the physical layer, which is a relatively common occurrence. Indeed, the eighth layer can be very challenging to troubleshoot. However, if it is kept in mind throughout the process of troubleshooting other layers, then layer eight issues may reveal themselves to the troubleshooter without the need to go through all the layers in between [18]. Common causes of layer eight issues include users who believe they are modifying a crucial setting to make something 'better' or 'faster,' without having the slightest understanding of what the setting actually does. This can cause such a wide array of problems that it is impossible to identify, mark, and list them on a piece of paper. It can be so devastating and disastrous that neither humans nor our implemented security mechanisms find any space to cope with such pressing issues, ultimately leading to the destruction of the communication medium, *i.e.*, the network.

4. SIMULATION RESULTS

While considering the abovementioned threats, there exists another layer named the "Eighth Layer". Further, there exists no research for assessing the security solutions individually. Therefore, this chapter intends to generate an evaluation criterion that tends to explain the security solutions employed and implemented at each level of the network. Thus, our research is focused on the parameter that evaluation of security assurance can be done on the index basis pertaining to any network which can be a mathematical function with respect to security indices. An example of a "Policy Layer" in Table **1**.

Table 1. An example of a policy layer.

S. No.	Parameter	Weightage
1	Performance of organization in a yearly audit of the adopted cyber security policy including regular and latest updates to software applications, Operating Systems, and their upgradation, use of antivirus measures, firewalls with effective rules, and other cyber security infrastructure. This audit should ideally be conducted by either an outside independent agency with expertise in cyber audit or an in-house dedicated section meant for this purpose only	25

(Table 1) cont.....

S. No.	Parameter	Weightage
2	Disciplinary actions and corrective actions are taken for violations reported in a year and on the cyber audit report	15
3	The organization owner has laid down a security policy or adopted an international state of art policy.	10
4	Periodical testing (*i.e.*, PT policy, Minimum yearly) of users in their understanding of the laid down policy is being carried out	10
5	Performance of users in the PT on policy	10
6	The ratio of the number of external employees (without administrative control of the organization's system) who use the system/network to the number of internal employees who use the system/network	10
7	Number of external audits carried out by the organization in five years	10
8	The ratio of the number of reported external employees	5
9	The ratio of the number of reported incidents to the number of system users in the organization	5

CONCLUSION

Recent studies in this field have led to the adoption of a holistic approach to Network Security. To promote this, extensive research is being conducted to analyze and model network flows. This chapter aims to introduce a new domain of Security Metrics. In the AAA CRISIL Grading, which assesses People, Processes, and Financial Soundness, there is no grading category for Information Security. Through this chapter, we aim to highlight a methodology that includes assessments by People, Processes, and Technology and introduces a grading system for these parameters to provide a straightforward mechanism for the grading of Information Networks.

REFERENCES

[1] S. Harini, K. Jothika, and K. Jayashree, "A survey on privacy and security in internet of things", *Int. J. Innov. Eng. Technol.,* vol. 8, no. 1, 2017.

[2] H. Mohammed, and M. Qayyum, "Internet of things: A study on security and privacy threats", *The 2nd International Conference on Anti-Cyber Crimes (ICACC) organized by IEEE,* 2017.

[3] Moussa Aboubakar, Mounir Kellil, and Pierre Roux, "A review of IoT network management: Current status and perspectives", *J. King. Saud. Univ. Comp.Inform.Sci.,* vol. 34, no. 7, pp. 4163-4176, 2022. [http://dx.doi.org/10.1016/j.jksuci.2021.03.006]

[4] NIST SP 800-64 Rev. A, Security Considerations in the Information System Development Life Cycle.

[5] Available from: http://gocsi.com/survey

[6] NIST SP 800-27 Rev A, Engineering Principles for Information Technology Security.

[7] NIST SP 800-42, Guidelines on Network Security Testing.

[8]   S. McClure, J. Scambray, and G. Kurtz, *Hacking Exposed.* 6th. McGraw-Hill Professional, 2009.

[9]   S. McClure, J. Scambray, and G. Kurtz, *Hacking Exposed.* 7th. McGraw-Hill Professional, 2012.

[10]   Available from: https://www.securitymetrics.com/blog/what-network-security

[11]   Saurabh Singhal, Amit Garg, and Shailendra Raj Tyagi, "A collective security metric for an information network", IJEMT, vol. 3, no. 2, 2015.

[12]   NIST SP 800 – 55 (Revision – 1).

[13]   ISO / IEC 27004 and ISO / IEC 15939.

[14]   Available   from: http://www.giac.org/paper/gsec/1641/implementing-network-security-metrics-programs/103004

[15]   Yan. Huang, and P. Yang, "Research of security metric architecture for next generation network", *Proceedings of IC : NIDC,* 2009.

[16]   K. Scarfone, and P. Mell, *The Common configuration scoring system (CCSS): Metrics for software security configuration vulnerabilities (Draft). Gaithersburg.* National Institute of Standards and Technology: MD, 2009.

[17]   M. Swanson, *Security self–assessment guide for information technology systems.* National Institute of Standards and Technology: Gaithersburg, MD, 2001.
        [http://dx.doi.org/10.6028/NIST.SP.800-26]

[18]   N. Seddigh, P. Pieda, A. Matrawy, B. Nandy, I. Labdadaris, and A. Hatfield, "Current trends and advances in information assurance metrics", *Proceedings of PST2004: The Second Annual Conference on Privacy, Security and Trust* Fredericton, NB, 2004.

SUBJECT INDEX

A

Accident 41
  alarm system 41
Accident detection 32, 34, 35, 36, 37, 38, 39,
    40, 41, 42, 48
  automatic 32, 39, 42
  automatic vehicle 48
  method 41
  system, automatic 34
Address resolution protocol (ARP) 120
Advanced encryption standard (AES) 117
Airbag system 40
Algorithms 18, 19, 20, 21, 22, 23, 24, 25, 41,
    74, 82, 86, 90, 91, 92, 94, 117, 121
  encryption 117, 121
  population-based 22
Amazon web services IoT 98
Ambulance driver 37
Ant colony optimization (ACO) 18, 22, 27
Antivirus measures 122
Ants, artificial 22
Applications 10, 11, 68, 81, 84, 85, 110
  home security 81
  intelligent mobility 110
  layer gateway (ALG) 84
  remote 68
  smart home 10, 85
  smartphone 84
  transportation 11
Architecture 4, 5, 6, 14, 86
Arduino-based air pollution monitoring
    system 13
Attribute-based encryption (ABE) 115
Audit 118, 122
  cyber 122
  onsite 118
Authentication, single-factor 118
Authorization, fingerprint 36
Automated 13, 82, 83
  electronic systems 13
  home system 82

system 83
Automatic 38, 48, 94
  accident detection techniques 38
  activation 48
  facial recognition system 94
Automation, exploiting progressive 108

B

Bacterial foraging algorithm (BFA) 18, 26
Behavior 9, 18, 73, 78, 96, 98
  environmental 18
Botnet activities in IoT-based applications 110
Brute force method 92
Business 96, 99, 100, 101, 102, 103, 104
  continuity plan 101
  impact analysis 101
  measures 102
  progression plans 102
  resilience 96, 99, 100, 103, 104
  works 101

C

Cameras 8, 41, 86
  dashboard 41
Capability, network safety 101
Capacity, restricted data transfer 114
Carbon monoxide 13
Cataclysmic events 101
Cloud 84, 97, 105, 115
  computing technologies 105
  IoT 97
  networking 84
  service providers (CSPs) 115
Cluster 50, 51, 52, 54, 55, 57, 58, 59, 60, 69,
    70, 71, 72, 75, 78
  based routing 52, 70
  distance 54, 57
  election 51
  formation 58, 59
  members (CMs) 51, 55, 57, 58, 59, 60, 78

www.ingramcontent.com/pod-product-compliance
Lightning Source LLC
Chambersburg PA
CBHW041715210326
41598CB00007B/657